AN AFRICAN Bite

CHEF MBOMBI

AN
AFRICAN
Bite

CHEF MBOMBI

Published in 2022 by Penguin Books
an imprint of Penguin Random House South Africa (Pty) Ltd
Company Reg. No. 1953/000441/07
The Estuaries, 4 Oxbow Crescent, Century Avenue, Century City 7441,
Cape Town, South Africa
PO Box 1144, Cape Town 8000, South Africa

www.penguinrandomhouse.co.za

ISBN 978-1-43231-124-7

Publisher: Beverley Dodd
Managing editor: Aimee Carelse
Designer: Randall Watson
Editor & indexer: Gill Gordon
Proofreader: Cecilia Barfield
Photographers: Henk Hattingh; Tshidiso "SkiGraphy" Lamola (page 128–129 and page 132)
Food stylist: Khanya Mzongwana
Stylist's assistant: Ellah Maepa

Reproduction by Studio Repro, Cape Town
Printed and bound in China by C&C Offset Printing Co., Ltd

MIX
Paper from
responsible sources
FSC® C018179
www.fsc.org

CONTENTS

Introduction

Producing my first cookbook is like a dream come true. Never in a million years could I have imagined this moment, where someone is holding my book. But here you are! I hope you enjoy reading it and, even more, that you will enjoy cooking from it.

This book is a reflection of my African-inspired cooking, full of dishes that will bring a feeling of nostalgia and connection to the place you call home. I hope my recipes remind you of the food that made you 'you', and bring back happy memories of the people who made that food – the joyful meals prepared by uGogo, uMama and noAuntie, or oMalume nabo Baba (uncles and fathers) who could never enjoy a meal without meat!

Food not only connects us to our heritage and culture, it plays a role in all life's great events. In joy we eat. In sorrow we eat. We eat to celebrate new life and to mourn those whose lives have ended. When we gather around the table we come together as one. Sharing food is an activity that unites families, friends and strangers. May these recipes recall happy family meals and informal gatherings, and the food you shared in both times of hardship and in good times.

I hope my book will be a bridge between our African culinary heritage and our busy modern lives. If we don't keep cooking the dishes we grew up with, the next generation may never know the pleasure of African food, made with love and served with pride.

DANIEL MBONANI MBOMBI

CHICKEN

Chicken Gizzards

Gizzards (amathumbu enkukhu) are the stomach of a chicken.
They can be tough, so long slow cooking is the answer. Frozen gizzards
are 'ready to cook' and just require rinsing after defrosting. In my toddler years,
there was a rhyme we used to sing when a chicken had been slaughtered.
It goes *'Amathumb' enkukhu amnandi nge papa' elishisayo'*.
Loosely translated, it means 'chicken gizzards go well with hot pap'!

PREP TIME	COOKING TIME	SERVES
10 MINUTES	**60** MINUTES	**4**

1 kg chicken gizzards, defrosted
2 Tbsp sunflower or canola oil
1 onion, finely chopped
2 garlic cloves, crushed
   or finely chopped
1 Tbsp chicken stock powder
   or 1 stock cube
250 ml water
Salt and black pepper to taste

1 Rinse the gizzards and pat dry with paper towel.
2 Heat the oil in a large pan. Add the gizzards, onion and garlic and fry for 10–15 minutes, until they are golden.
3 Crumble over the stock powder. Add the water and salt and pepper to taste, and simmer over medium heat, stirring frequently, for about 40 minutes, until the gizzards are tender and the gravy has thickened. Serve hot, with freshly made hot pap.

Umleqwa

Umleqwa, fondly known as hardbody chickens, were the original free-range birds, roaming the streets of every township and village. Even today, you'll still find them in yards in urban townships. They remind us of when our grandmothers or mothers would passionately prepare umleqwa with dumplings (idombolo) for any long distance trip. On Sundays, umleqwa would be the star of a Seven Colours feast. I call this dish my 'genesis' as it holds fond memories for me, and I still enjoy cooking and eating it.

BOILED CHICKEN PIECES

PREP TIME	COOKING TIME	SERVES
5 MINUTES	1.5 HOURS	4

1 chicken, cut into 8 pieces
Salt and black pepper to taste
1 medium onion, chopped
3 garlic cloves, crushed or finely chopped
1 litre water

1 Season the chicken with salt and pepper and place in a single layer in a large pot. Add the onion and garlic, and water to cover (you need a large pot to allow the chicken to cook evenly).
2 Simmer on medium to medium-low heat for 1½ hours, or until the meat is tender. Serve with steamed bread, boiled potatoes, or pap.

See photographs on pages 14–15.

SPICY CHICKEN PIECES

PREP TIME	COOKING TIME	SERVES
5–10 MINUTES	1.5 HOURS	4

1 chicken, cut into 8 pieces
1–2 tsp ground paprika
1–2 tsp cayenne pepper
1 medium onion, chopped
3 garlic cloves, crushed or finely chopped
2 green chillies, seeds removed and chopped
1 litre water
3–4 medium potatoes, washed, peeled and cut into quarters (optional)
1 Tbsp butter (optional)

1 Season the chicken with paprika and cayenne pepper. Place the chicken in a single layer in a large pot. Add the onion, garlic and chillies and water to cover.
2 Simmer on medium to medium-low heat for 1½ hours or until the meat is tender (topping up with a little boiling water if necessary).
3 After 60 minutes, add the potatoes and butter, if using. The potatoes will be done when they are soft when pierced with a knife. Serve with pap or steamed bread.

SPICY CHICKEN PIECES (BELOW) AND BOILED CHICKEN PIECES (RIGHT), *SEE PAGE 13.*

Chef's tip

A home-reared hardbody chicken needs time to cook. If you use supermarket chicken, reduce the total cooking time to 60 minutes (add the potatoes after 30 minutes).

Braaied Chicken Wings

This is absolutely everyone's favourite snack! This quantity makes three starter portions, but you can easily increase it to feed a crowd.

PREP TIME

10 MINUTES
+ 1 hour marinating time

COOKING TIME

20 MINUTES
over prepared coals

SERVES

3

12 wings
Salt and black pepper to taste

SWEET CHILLI MARINADE
100 ml sweet chilli sauce
2 Tbsp olive oil
2 garlic cloves, crushed
  or finely chopped
2 Tbsp grated Parmesan
  or Parmesan-style cheese
1 Tbsp coriander seeds, crushed
1 Tbsp garlic powder
1 tsp cayenne powder
½ tsp dried parsley
½ tsp dried thyme

1 Rinse the wings and pat dry with paper towel. Season to taste with salt and pepper.
2 Combine the marinade ingredients in a bowl. Add the wings, turning them until they are well coated. Cover with cling wrap and place in the fridge for at least 1 hour.
3 Prepare the braai so the coals are hot but not smoky. Braai the wings for 15–20 minutes, turning once or twice and brushing with the marinade. (Take care that they do not burn.)

Chef's tips

- To cook the chicken in the oven, place the wings on a baking sheet and cook at 180°C for about 20 minutes, until golden brown, brushing with the marinade after 10 minutes.
- To cook the chicken on a kettle braai, prepare the coals for indirect and direct cooking over medium heat. Braai the wings over direct heat for 4–5 minutes, with the lid closed, turning once. Move the wings to indirect heat and cook for 15–20 minutes, brushing with reserved marinade in the last 10 minutes. Keep the lid closed as much as possible to avoid losing too much heat.
- When scaling up the quantities, don't add too much cayenne pepper; rather increase it by ½–1 tsp at a time.
- Take care when using marinade from raw chicken. If you baste the chicken within 5–10 minutes, the heat from the cooking process will make it safe. If you want to use the marinade to glaze cooked chicken just before serving, it must first be boiled for 3–4 minutes (on the stove or in the microwave) to destroy any harmful bacteria.

Chicken Neck Stew

The nice thing about chicken is that just about every part of it is edible, besides its feathers. Chicken necks are an easy dish to cook and make a great snack as well. Here's how I do it.

PREP TIME

10 MINUTES

COOKING TIME

40 MINUTES

SERVES

4

+ 20 minutes marinating time

1 kg chicken necks
1 tsp ground paprika
1 tsp onion powder
1 tsp garlic powder
Salt and black pepper to taste
3–4 Tbsp canola oil
  or sunflower oil
1 medium onion, chopped
4 garlic cloves, crushed
  or finely chopped
1 Tbsp tomato paste
500 ml chicken stock

1 Rinse the chicken necks, pat dry and place in a bowl. Add the paprika, onion powder, garlic powder and salt and pepper to taste and toss to coat. Set aside for 20 minutes.

2 Heat 1–2 Tbsp oil in a large pan on high heat and fry the necks for 5–10 minutes, then set aside while you prepare the sauce.

3 Add the remaining oil to the pan. Lower the heat and fry the onion and garlic until softened and golden brown. Add the tomato paste and stir through.

4 Return the chicken necks to the pan along with the stock and simmer for 20 minutes, until the sauce thickens. Serve with pap or warm garlic bread.

Chicken Hearts
WITH BACON

A hearty and delightful stew made with the simplest of ingredients but meant to tickle the tummy and, of course, touch the heart. Chicken hearts are amongst my favourites for their succulent texture and ability to blend with just about anything, including chicken gizzards or livers. I add a twist and play with bacon.

PREP TIME

10 MINUTES

COOKING TIME

20–30 MINUTES

SERVES
4

+ 1 hour marinating time

1 kg chicken hearts

4 garlic cloves, crushed or finely chopped

4 green or red chillies, finely chopped

1 Tbsp fresh ginger, peeled and finely chopped

½ tsp black pepper

½ tsp dried thyme

½ tsp dried basil

½ tsp ground paprika

Salt to taste

2 Tbsp cooking oil

800 g streaky bacon, chopped

125 ml BBQ sauce

1 Rinse the chicken hearts, pat dry and place in a bowl. Add the garlic, chillies, ginger, black pepper, thyme, basil, paprika and salt to taste. Add the oil and stir through, then set aside for 1 hour, to marinate.

2 Preheat a pan on medium high. Add the marinated hearts and bacon and cook, stirring occasionally, for about 20 minutes. Turn off the heat, stir in the BBQ sauce and cook for a further 5 minutes. Serve with crusty bread, rice or pap.

Chef's tips

- Short of time? Use 1 tsp each of ready chopped fresh garlic, ginger and chillies.
- Choose regular paprika or smoked paprika.

Chicken Livers

What's a starter menu without chicken livers, or a chicken chapter without them? Chicken livers are easy to cook, but the trick is not to overcook them unless you want a paste-like consistency!

PREP TIME

10 MINUTES

+ 1 hour marinating time

COOKING TIME

20 MINUTES

SERVES

4

as a starter or 2 as a main course

1 kg fresh chicken livers
2 Tbsp canola oil or sunflower oil
1 onion, finely chopped
4 garlic cloves, crushed
  or finely chopped
1 tsp ground paprika
1 tsp garlic powder
1 tsp onion powder
1 can (400 g) chopped tomatoes
2–3 Tbsp grated Parmesan
  or Parmesan-style cheese
Fresh basil, for garnish

1 Rinse the chicken livers and pat dry, then set aside.
2 Heat the oil in a pan over high heat and fry the onion and garlic until golden. Season the chicken livers with paprika, garlic powder and onion powder and add to the pan. Fry until just browned on all sides, about 10 minutes. (Don't overcrowd the pan; rather cook the livers in two batches if necessary.)
3 Add the chopped tomatoes and cheese. Stir through, and cook for a further 2 minutes. (The livers should still be pink in the centre.) Scatter over the basil and serve hot, with warm garlic bread.

Chef's tips

• If you use frozen chicken livers, make sure they are fully thawed beforehand.
• For a bit of heat, substitute a can of Mexican- or Indian-style chopped tomatoes, and add a thinly sliced fresh red chilli or 1–2 tsp chilli flakes, and/or a dash of your favourite hot sauce.

Stovetop Chicken Stew

Absolutely no home in Mzansi is complete without a recipe for ama-pieces, aka chicken pieces. This tasty go-to dish can be eaten with just about anything: pap, rice, chips or mash. Great for any day of the week.

PREP TIME
10 MINUTES

COOKING TIME
60 MINUTES

SERVES
3–4

2 Tbsp butter

1 onion, chopped

2 garlic cloves, crushed
   or chopped

2 carrots, chopped

1 Tbsp flour

8 chicken pieces

250 g baby potatoes

300 ml chicken stock

1 tsp chicken spice

1. Heat the butter in a large pan over medium-high heat and fry the onion and garlic until soft.
2. Add the carrots and stir to coat. Sprinkle over the flour and continue frying for about 5 minutes, then remove the veggies and set aside.
3. Add the chicken pieces to the pan skin-side down, and fry, turning often, until golden brown on all sides, about 20 minutes.
4. Return the veggies to the pan, along with the baby potatoes, chicken stock and chicken spice. Reduce the heat to medium and cook for about 30 minutes, until the chicken is cooked through and the potatoes are tender when pierced with a skewer.

Chef's tip

- Ama-pieces refers to a whole chicken that has been cut into at least eight pieces (often called a 'braai pack'). If you prefer, you can use an 8-piece thighs-and-drums pack; just don't call it ama-pieces!

Beef Stew

WITH CARROTS AND THYME

Beef stew is high on my list of comfort foods, it's easy to make and can enjoyed with just about any starch. I like it best with rice or pap. Like all stews, it's even better when made ahead and reheated, giving the flavours time to develop.

PREP TIME	COOKING TIME	SERVES
10 MINUTES	60 MINUTES	4

1 kg cubed beef

2 Tbsp Maizena or flour, for dusting

2–3 Tbsp canola oil or sunflower oil

1 red onion, roughly chopped

1–2 carrots, roughly chopped

4 garlic cloves, chopped or sliced

4–5 sprigs fresh thyme

8–10 fresh basil leaves, chopped

Salt and ground black pepper
   to taste

4 tsp beef stock powder
   or 3–4 stock cubes

1 litre boiling water

1 Dust the meat with flour. Heat the oil in a pot over medium heat and fry the beef cubes for 20 minutes, until browned on all sides. Remove from the pot and set aside.

2 Add a little more oil to the pot, if needed. Add the onion, carrots and garlic and cook for 2–3 minutes, until softened. Add the thyme, basil, and salt and pepper to taste, and fry for 5 minutes, until the onion is golden brown.

3 Return the meat into the pot and add the stock powder and water. Lower the heat and simmer until the liquid reduces and meat is tender, about 35 minutes. Serve with pap or mashed potato.

Chef's tips

- For extra flavour, substitute the Maizena or flour with 1 Tbsp oxtail soup powder. Don't neglect to dust the meat before browning, as the flour or soup powder helps to thicken the stew.
- Instead of fresh herbs, you can use 1–2 tsp each dried thyme and basil.

Oxtail *and* Potato Stew

All I can say is, 'Oh my tummy!'. This satisfying and comforting dish is perfect for cold days. It takes a while to cook, but the delectable aromas coming from the kitchen will make you wish it was dinner time already!

PREP TIME
10–15 MINUTES

COOKING TIME
2½ HOURS

SERVES
4

2–3 Tbsp canola oil or sunflower oil

1 kg oxtail

1 onion, chopped

4 garlic cloves, crushed
   or finely chopped

3 Tbsp Maizena, flour
   or oxtail soup powder

1 tsp onion powder

1 tsp garlic powder

1 tsp ground paprika

1 tsp dried parsley

4 tsp beef stock powder
   or 3–4 stock cubes

1 litre boiling water

500 g potatoes, peeled
   and cut into chunks

Salt and ground black pepper
   to taste

1 Heat the oil in an ovenproof pot or casserole dish, over medium-high heat, and brown the oxtail for about 20 minutes. Add the onion and garlic, sprinkle over the flour and continue to brown for another 10–15 minutes.

2 Add the onion powder, garlic powder, smoked paprika and dried parsley. Stir through and continue to cook for another 10 minutes. (Add a little water if it starts to burn.)

3 Add the stock powder and water, stir though and cook for 2–3 minutes more.

4 Cover the dish with a lid and place in a preheated oven at 180°C. Cook for 1 hour, then add the potatoes and cook for another 30 minutes, with the lid on, until the potatoes are tender when pierced with a skewer and the meat is almost falling off the bones, and you have a thick gravy. Season to taste.

5 Serve with dumplings, rice or mashed potatoes.

Chef's tip

• Instead of cooking the dish in the oven, you can continue to cook the oxtail on the stovetop, over a medium heat and with the lid on, for the same amount of time.

Boerewors Stew

You can never go wrong with wors; it's an affordable, go-to meat.
You can have this dish alone or with a starch of your choice.

PREP TIME

10
MINUTES

COOKING TIME

50
MINUTES

SERVES

4

500 g baby potatoes

2 carrots, peeled and cut
   into chunks

Canola oil or sunflower oil,
   for cooking

1 kg boerewors or beef sausage,
   cut into finger-sized pieces

1 onion, finely chopped

4–5 garlic cloves, thinly sliced

2 tsp stock powder

500 ml boiling water

2 Tbsp Maizena
   or beef soup powder

½ cup freshly chopped parsley

Salt and ground black pepper
   to taste

1 Boil the baby potatoes and carrots separately in salted water until just tender, then drain and set aside.

2 Meanwhile, heat some oil in a large pan over medium heat and fry the sausage for about 10 minutes, until cooked through. Remove from the pan and set aside.

3 Increase the heat to high. Add the onion and garlic to the pan (adding a bit more oil, if necessary), and fry for about 5 minutes, until golden brown.

4 Lower the heat to medium. Dissolve the stock powder in the boiling water. Return the sausage, plus any juices, to the pan, along with the potatoes and carrots. Add the hot stock and simmer for 30 minutes.

5 Sprinkle over the Maizena or soup powder and stir in, along with most of the parsley (reserve some for garnish) and simmer for 2–3 minutes, until the sauce thickens. Scatter over the remainder of the parsley. Serve with rice.

Chef's tips

- To create individual sausages, twist the boerewors into links (10–12 cm long) and use kitchen scissors or a sharp knife to cut between them.
- When cooking sausage, use tongs rather than a fork to prevent piercing the skin, which causes the juices to run out, making the meat tougher.

Lamb Trotters
AND CHICKPEA CURRY

I learnt this recipe from an Indian friend. Served with warm rotis, it's a filling comfort-food dish for a winter's evening. You can vary the heat by choosing a milder or hotter curry paste and curry powder; the choice is yours.

PREP TIME	COOKING TIME	SERVES
15 MINUTES	**80** MINUTES	**4**

+ 1½ hours to precook the trotters

TROTTERS

1 kg lamb trotters
1–2 tsp salt
1 tsp black pepper
4 tsp beef stock powder
1 litre boiling water

CURRY

4 Tbsp canola oil or sunflower oil
1 onion, chopped
4 garlic cloves, crushed or chopped
1 Tbsp ginger paste
1 Tbsp curry paste
1 Tbsp curry powder
2 tsp garlic powder
2 tsp onion powder
1 can (400 g) chickpeas, drained and rinsed
Fresh coriander leaves, for garnish

TO COOK THE TROTTERS

1 Season with salt and pepper and place in a deep pot. Add the stock powder and water to cover (you may not need the full litre) and cook over a medium heat until the meat is tender, about 1½ hours.

2 Remove the trotters with a slotted spoon and set aside. Retain the cooking broth.

TO MAKE THE CURRY

1 Heat the oil in a pot over low heat and fry the onion, garlic, ginger paste and curry paste for about 5 minutes.

2 Stir in the curry powder, garlic powder and onion powder and cook for 1–2 minutes.

3 Add the trotters plus their cooking broth and cook over a medium heat for about 60 minutes, until the broth reduces and thickens.

4 Add the chickpeas, stir gently, and cook for a further 5–10 minutes. Garnish with fresh coriander leaves and serve with warm rotis.

Chef's tip

• Instead of fresh garlic, use 2 Tbsp ready-made garlic and ginger paste.

Marinated Lamb Chops

I am yet to meet anyone (besides vegans!) who doesn't like lamb chops.
They're easy to prepare but there is something 'special occasion' about them.
Maybe it's because of the price! Once marinated, the chops can be pan-fried,
grilled or cooked on the braai, but however you choose to cook them,
garlic bread makes a great accompaniment.

PREP TIME **COOKING TIME** **SERVES**

10 MINUTES

10 MINUTES

4

+ 1 hour
marinating time

1 kg lamb chops
Salt and black pepper to taste
1–2 Tbsp canola oil, olive oil
   or sunflower oil, for cooking

MARINADE

2 Tbsp olive oil
2 Tbsp light soy sauce
4 garlic cloves, crushed
   or finely chopped
½ cup chopped fresh rosemary
½ cup chopped fresh thyme
1 Tbsp dried mint

1. Combine the marinade ingredients in a non-metallic dish. Season the chops with salt and pepper.
2. Add the chops to the marinade, turning to coat, then cover and set aside for 1 hour, or overnight in the fridge. (Allow the chops to come to room temperature before cooking.)
3. Heat 1–2 Tbsp oil in a pan. Fry the chops for 3–4 minutes on each side for medium to well-done. Allow to rest for 1–2 minutes before serving.

Chef's tips

- To grill the chops, place them on a rack under a preheated grill and cook for 3–4 minutes on each side. If preferred, braai the chops over medium coals for 3–4 minutes on each side.
- Instead of soy sauce, you can use Worcestershire sauce in the marinade.

Lamb *and* Bacon Stew

This fragrant, tasty lamb stew makes a perfect dinner on a cold winter's night.

PREP TIME

5–10
MINUTES

COOKING TIME

40
MINUTES

SERVES

4

½ cup flour
Salt and black pepper to taste
½ tsp dried thyme
1 kg deboned lamb, cubed
1–2 Tbsp olive oil
500 g streaky bacon, chopped
1 onion, chopped
3 garlic cloves, crushed
   or finely chopped
2 tsp beef stock powder
500 ml boiling water
1 Tbsp tomato paste
2 bay leaves

1 Combine the flour, salt and pepper and dried thyme in a bowl. Add the lamb and toss gently to coat. Set aside.

2 Heat the oil in a pot over medium heat and fry the bacon, onion and garlic for about 2 minutes.

3 Add the seasoned lamb and fry for a further 5 minutes, until browned all over.

4 Dissolve the stock powder in the boiling water. Stir in the tomato paste, then add the stock and bay leaves to the pot. Cover with a lid and simmer for 35 minutes. About 5 minutes before the end of the cooking time, remove the lid and increase the heat, to allow the gravy to reduce and thicken. Serve with pap, mashed potatoes or rice.

Ox Tripe – Three Ways

Tripe is one of the most revered dishes in Mzansi, and across the continent. Although tripe takes time to prepare, it can be an uncomplicated dish, given how minimalist the ingredients are, and many people enjoy it most when it is cooked plainly. But, because we all have different tastes, I've also given you recipes for a classic curried tripe and a contemporary version with Mediterranean flavours.

BASIC BOILED TRIPE AND INTESTINES

PREP TIME	COOKING TIME	SERVES
5 MINUTES	**3** HOURS	**4**

1 kg clean ox tripe, cubed
1 kg clean intestines, cubed
3 litres water plus 2 Tbsp salt
Salt and ground black pepper
  to taste
Chilli powder to taste, optional

1 Ensure the tripe and intestines are thoroughly washed. Place in a pot with salted water to cover. Bring to a boil and cook for about 3 hours, until soft (adding more boiling water if necessary), then drain.

2 Season with salt and pepper to taste (and a sprinkling of chilli powder, if you like). Serve with uphuthu (pap), or use for one of the following recipes.

Chef's tip

- To save time when preparing these recipes, boil the tripe a day ahead. (To cook 1 kg tripe on its own, follow the basic recipe, reducing the amount of salted water by half.)

CURRIED TRIPE

PREP TIME
10 MINUTES

COOKING TIME
35 MINUTES

SERVES
4

(With pre-cooked tripe)

2–3 Tbsp canola oil
  or sunflower oil
1 onion chopped
1–2 garlic cloves, crushed
  or finely chopped
1 kg cooked, cubed tripe
  (*see* opposite)
2 Tbsp curry paste
1 Tbsp garam masala

1 Tbsp black pepper
½ tsp ground coriander
½ tsp ground cumin
½ tsp ground paprika
½ tsp cayenne pepper
1 can chopped tomatoes
4 tsp beef stock powder
  or 3–4 stock cubes
500 ml boiling water

1 Heat the oil in a pot and fry the onion and garlic for 2–3 minutes, until soft.
2 Add the cooked tripe, curry paste, garam masala, black pepper and all the spices, and stir to combine. Cook, stirring occasionally, on medium heat for about 20 minutes.
3 Add the tomatoes, stock powder or cubes and water and continue cooking for 10 minutes, until the sauce thickens. Serve with warm rotis or freshly made pap.

TRIPE AND CHORIZO

PREP TIME
10 MINUTES

COOKING TIME
40 MINUTES

SERVES
4

(With pre-cooked tripe)

2–3 Tbsp canola oil
  or sunflower oil
1 kg chorizo, cubed
1 onion, chopped
5 garlic cloves, crushed
  or finely chopped
1 kg cooked cubed tripe
  (*see* opposite)
2–3 tsp black pepper
½ tsp dried thyme

½ tsp garlic flakes
½ tsp dried parsley
½ tsp onion flakes
½ tsp ground paprika
½ tsp cayenne pepper
½ tsp dried origanum
2 Tbsp tomato paste
2 tsp beef stock powder
  or 2–3 stock cubes
500 ml boiling water

1 Heat the oil in a pot and fry the chorizo, onion and garlic for 5 minutes until the onions are soft.
2 Add the cooked tripe and all the herbs and spices and stir to coat. Stir in the tomato paste.
3 Cook, stirring occasionally, on medium heat, for 10 minutes.
4 Add the stock powder or cubes and water and continue cooking for 25 minutes, until the sauce thickens. Serve with warm rotis or garlic bread.

TRIPE AND CHORIZO (BELOW)
AND CURRIED TRIPE (OPPOSITE), SEE PAGE 39.

Ox Liver
WITH BACON AND JALAPEÑOS

In Zulu, if you are teased about how brave you are, we say *'unesibindi'*, loosely translated as 'You have a liver of an ox'. Hence we say: 'Never translate Zulu!' Anyway, ox liver is one of my favourite delicacies any day. It's easy to make, too. (It's also the ideal breakfast dish to deal with last night's hangover!)

PREP TIME
10 MINUTES

COOKING TIME
30 MINUTES

SERVES
4

+ 1 hour marinating time

1 kg ox liver, cubed
500 g streaky bacon, chopped
6–8 jalapeños, thinly sliced
4 garlic cloves, crushed
  or finely chopped
2 spring onions, thinly sliced
2 tsp BBQ spice
½ tsp ground paprika
½ tsp brown sugar
½ tsp mustard powder
½ tsp garlic powder
½ tsp celery salt
Salt and black pepper to taste
3 Tbsp canola oil or sunflower oil
3 Tbsp BBQ sauce

1 Place the cubed liver in a bowl with the bacon, jalapeños, garlic, spring onions and all the seasonings. Add 1 Tbsp oil and stir to combine. Set aside for 1 hour to marinate.

2 Heat the remaining oil in a pan on medium high. Add the liver and bacon mixture and fry for 20–25 minutes, stirring occasionally, to prevent it from catching.

3 Stir in the BBQ sauce and cook for a further 3 minutes, stirring occasionally. Serve with pap, rotis or garlic bread.

Chef's tips

• To really bring out the flavours, place the marinated liver in the fridge for 3–4 hours, or overnight.

• If you prefer less heat, remove the seeds from the jalapeños and/or omit the cayenne pepper. For an added kick, replace the BBQ sauce with your favourite sweet chilli sauce.

• You can also make this with 500 g chicken livers, roughly chopped.

Ox Heart and Lungs

Fresh heart and lungs become available when an ox or cow is slaughtered in a ritual ceremony. Some township butchers sell prepacked heart and lungs, but you might have difficulty finding them in suburban supermarkets.

 PREP TIME 5–10 MINUTES
+ 1 hour marinating time

 COOKING TIME 50 MINUTES

 SERVES 4

500 g ox heart, cubed

500 g ox lung, cubed

2 Tbsp canola oil or sunflower oil

2 tsp beef stock powder
    or 1–2 stock cubes

500 ml boiling water

1 onion, thinly sliced

1 red pepper, thinly sliced

1 tsp ground paprika

1 tsp cayenne pepper

½ tsp chilli powder

Salt and black pepper to taste

1 Rinse the meat and pat dry. Heat the oil in a pot on high heat. Add the cubed meat and fry for 1–2 minutes, until just brown.

2 Add the stock powder and boiling water. Lower the heat to medium and simmer for 30–40 minutes, until tender.

3 Add the onion, red pepper, spices, and salt and pepper to taste, and cook for a further 10 minutes, until the onion and red pepper are soft. Serve with pap or brown bread.

Chef's tips

• Organ meat has a shorter shelf life than the rest of the carcass, so always make sure it is fresh when you buy it, and cook it within a day or two.

• Instead of using heart and lungs, use 1 kg heart meat.

Goat Meat Stew

In Zulu tradition, goats are slaughtered for most ancestral rituals and social ceremonies, including marriages and burials. Because goat meat can be hard to find in the city, most people only eat it as part of a ceremony. But if you can find some, goat meat makes a great meal. (Fresh goat's milk is good, too.)

PREP TIME 10 MINUTES **COOKING TIME** 90 MINUTES **SERVES** 4

2 kg goat meat, chopped into serving-size pieces
1 onion, chopped
4 garlic cloves, crushed or very finely chopped
1–2 celery stalks (stem and leaves), rougly chopped
1 bouquet garni, *see* Chef's tip
1 Tbsp each salt and black pepper
4 tsp beef stock powder or 3–4 beef stock cubes
1 litre boiling water

1 Place the goat meat in a pot along with the chopped onion, garlic, celery, bouquet garni and salt and pepper.
2 Add the stock powder or cubes and enough boiling water to cover (you may not need the full amount).
3 Simmer on medium heat for 80–90 minutes, until the liquid has reduced to a thick gravy and the meat is tender. Before serving, remove the celery stalks and the bouquet garni. Serve with soft pap.

Chef's tips

- To develop even more flavour, heat some oil in the pot and brown the meat on all sides for 3–4 minutes before adding the other ingredients.
- A bouquet garni is a small bunch of fresh herbs tied with string, which is removed before serving. For this dish, combine 2–3 sprigs of fresh thyme, 3–4 sprigs of fresh parsley and 1 dried bay leaf. Instead of fresh herbs, use 2 tsp each dried thyme and parsley, and 1 dried bay leaf.

FISH

Beer-battered Hake

PREP TIME
5 MINUTES

+ 30 minutes chilling time

COOKING TIME
5–10 MINUTES

SERVES
6

BEER BATTER

1 cup (250 ml) flour
1 tsp baking powder
½ tsp onion flakes
½ tsp garlic flakes
½ tsp black pepper
½ tsp salt
340 ml beer
1 large egg, lightly beaten

HAKE

6 hake fillets, defrosted if frozen
Canola oil or sunflower oil,
  for cooking

TO MAKE THE BATTER

1 Combine the flour, baking powder, onion flakes, garlic flakes, black pepper and salt in a large bowl.
2 Make a well in the centre and gradually add the beer whilst whisking, then add the beaten egg and whisk to create a smooth batter. (Instead of whisking by hand, you can use a hand-held blender.) Chill the batter in the fridge for 30 minutes before frying the fish.

TO COOK THE FISH

1 Heat the oil in a saucepan on high heat. Dip the hake fillets, one at a time, into the batter and place in the pan. Deep-fry for 3–4 minutes, until golden brown. To avoid lowering the temperature of the oil too much, cook just one or two fillets at a time.
2 Place the fried fish on paper towel to drain any excess oil. Keep warm while you cook the remaining fish. Serve hot, with chips.

Baked Hake

WITH OLIVES, TOMATOES, PEPPADEWS, GARLIC & CHILLI

PREP TIME
5 MINUTES
+ 30 minutes chilling time

COOKING TIME
5-8 MINUTES

SERVES
6

6 hake fillets, defrosted if frozen
½ tsp salt
½ tsp pepper
1 cup olives, pitted and chopped
1 cup cherry tomatoes, halved
1 cup Peppadews® (mild piquanté peppers) drained and chopped
2 garlic cloves, crushed or finely chopped
2 fresh chillies, finely chopped
½ cup fresh basil, finely chopped
½ cup fresh coriander, finely chopped
2 Tbsp olive oil
1–2 Tbsp lemon juice

1 Place the fish in a single layer in an ovenproof dish. Season with salt and pepper, scatter over the remaining ingredients and drizzle with olive oil and lemon juice to taste. Cover the dish and place in the fridge for 30 minutes to marinate. Remove from the fridge 10–15 minutes before cooking, to allow it to come to room temperature.

2 Preheat the oven to 180°C. Bake for 5–8 minutes, until the fish is cooked through and flakes easily.

Deep fried Fish Bones

One of the simplest yet most delectable treats of my childhood was fish bones.
After a whole fish was filleted, mom would fry the bones separately.
They made the perfect weekday snack.

PREP TIME

5 MINUTES

COOKING TIME
5 MINUTES

SERVES
4

8 fish bones

2 Tbsp flour

½ tsp salt

1 Tbsp black pepper

Finely grated zest of 1 lemon

4 cups canola oil or sunflower oil,
   for cooking

Lemon wedges, for serving

1 Rinse the fish bones and pat dry with paper towel
   (if the bones are wet, the flour won't stick). Combine the
   flour, salt, pepper and lemon zest in a bowl. Add the bones
   to the seasoned flour and toss to coat.

2 Heat the oil in a deep saucepan and deep-fry the bones
   for 3–5 minutes, until golden brown. Drain on paper towel
   and serve hot, with a squeeze of lemon juice.

Braaied Tilapia

PREP TIME
5-10 MINUTES

+ marinating time

COOKING TIME
20 MINUTES

SERVES
4

2–3 whole tilapia or line fish

Juice of 2 lemons

4 shallots or 1 medium onion, finely chopped

2 Tbsp olive oil

1 cup fresh parsley, chopped

1 cup fresh chives, chopped

1 Tbsp ground black pepper

1 Tbsp white pepper

1 Tbsp crushed garlic

1 Tbsp ground paprika

1 Rinse the fish and pat dry with paper towel. Using a sharp knife, score four lines across the fish. Squeeze over the lemon juice, ensuring the fish is evenly coated.

2 Place the remaining ingredients in a blender and pulse to a paste. (If necessary, add just enough water to make it spreadable.) Spread the paste on both sides of the fish then place in a non-metallic dish, cover with cling wrap, and marinate in the fridge for 60 minutes, or up to 8 hours. Remove the fish from the fridge 10–15 minutes before cooking, to allow it to come to room temperature.

3 Place the tilapia in hinged braai grid to ensure it won't fall apart as you turn it. Braai over medium coals for 4–5 minutes per side, turning once, until the flesh is opaque and flakes easily. Serve with couscous or baby potatoes, with lemon wedges on the side.

Chef's tips

• To pan-fry, preheat a little oil in a ridged grill pan over medium heat and cook the fish for 4–5 minutes per side until the flesh is opaque and flakes easily.

• To prevent the fish from sticking on the braai, spray the grid with nonstick cooking spray before cooking.

Braaied Snoek
AND PEACHES WITH HERB MAYO

When it comes to braaied fish, snoek is the queen! This dish is a great choice for a relaxed Saturday afternoon with family or friends.

PREP TIME
5–10 MINUTES

COOKING TIME
20–30 MINUTES

SERVES
4

± 1–2 hours marinating time

1 whole snoek (± 1 kg)
2–3 Tbsp olive oil
1 Tbsp black pepper
1 Tbsp biltong spice or braai spice
½ tsp salt
1 lemon, thinly sliced
4 ripe peaches or nectarines
1–2 Tbsp olive oil
Ground black pepper to taste

HERB MAYO

2 cups (500 ml) mayonnaise
2–3 Tbsp lemon juice
Fresh parsley, finely chopped
Fresh basil, finely chopped
1 Tbsp black pepper
2 tsp truffle oil, optional

1 Using a sharp knife, make three or four diagonal cuts in the skin of the snoek.

2 Combine the olive oil, pepper, biltong spice or braai spice and salt in a small bowl and rub all over the fish. Place the lemon slices inside the snoek. Leave to chill in fridge for 1–2 hours.

3 When ready to cook, prepare the braai with medium-hot coals. Place the snoek on an oiled braai grid and cook for 10–15 minutes per side.

4 Halve the peaches and remove the stones. Brush lightly with olive oil and season with black pepper. When you turn the snoek, place the peaches on the grid, skin-side down. After about 5 minutes, turn them to give the flesh some grill marks. (Prepare the peaches at the last minute, to prevent them from discolouring.)

TO MAKE THE HERB MAYO

1. Place the mayonnaise in a mixing bowl with the lemon juice, chopped herbs and black pepper. Stir to combine. Check the seasoning, scoop into a serving bowl and place in the fridge until ready to serve. Just before serving, drizzle over the truffle oil.

Chef's tips
- Defrost frozen snoek according to the package instructions.
- Instead of truffle oil, use 1–2 tsp garlic-, chilli-, lemon-, or basil-flavoured oil to flavour the mayonnaise.

Canned Pilchards
IN HOMEMADE TOMATO SAUCE

A definite Mzansi favourite – from the suburbs to the 'hood – pilchards are enjoyed with just about anything. Their simplicity makes them a favourite in our homes. My recipe takes the humble can of pilchards to a whole new level!

PREP TIME	COOKING TIME	SERVES
5 MINUTES	15 MINUTES	2

3 Tbsp canola oil or sunflower oil

1 onion, finely chopped

2 garlic cloves, crushed
   or finely chopped

3 tomatoes, finely chopped

½ tsp ground paprika

½ tsp garlic powder

½ tsp onion powder

1 can (400 g) pilchards in
   tomato sauce

100 ml chicken stock (1 tsp stock
   powder plus 100 ml boiling water)

Salt and black pepper to taste

1 Heat the oil in a pan over medium heat. Add the onion and garlic and fry for about 2 minutes, until just golden.

2 Add the tomatoes, paprika, garlic powder and onion powder and simmer for about 10 minutes.

3 Drain the pilchards, reserving the sauce. Add the pilchards to the pan, along with the stock and salt and pepper. Cook for 2 minutes, then add the reserved sauce and simmer for a further 2 minutes, until the sauce thickens a bit. Serve with pap, rice or bread.

Pan-fried Salmon
WITH HONEY-SOY MARINADE

Salmon is the 'rich auntie' of the fish family. She doesn't require much, but when dressed up with just the right accessories, she knows how to give her best. Here, Asian flavours delight the palate in what is surely a special occasion meal.

PREP TIME **5** MINUTES
+ marinating time

COOKING TIME **4–5** MINUTES

SERVES **2**

2 salmon portions (± 200 g each)
2 Tbsp olive oil, for cooking

HONEY-SOY MARINADE
½ cup (125 ml) honey
3–4 Tbsp dark soy sauce
1 Tbsp olive oil
4 garlic cloves, crushed
  or very finely chopped
2 Tbsp finely crushed ginger
1 tsp ground black pepper

1 Combine the marinade ingredients in a shallow dish. Add the salmon portions, turn to coat, and set aside for 1 hour, to marinade.

2 Heat some olive oil in a pan over medium heat. Remove the salmon from the marinade and place, skin-side down in the pan. Cook for for 2–3 minutes, then turn and cook for a further 2 minutes, until the flesh is opaque and flakes easily.

3 Meanwhile, pour the marinade into a small saucepan and bring boiling point. Serve the salmon with fried potato slices, baby potatoes or mashed potatoes and drizzle over some of the warm marinade.

Oven-baked Sardines

Served whole, these tasty little fish make a quick and easy meal.

PREP TIME
5 MINUTES

COOKING TIME
6–8 MINUTES

SERVES
2

+ 1 hour marinating time

8 whole sardines

½ tsp sea salt, plus extra for serving

1 Tbsp black pepper, plus extra for serving

6 garlic cloves, crushed or very thinly sliced

3–4 Tbsp olive oil

1–2 Tbsp lemon juice, plus lemon wedges for serving

1 Season the sardines, inside and out, with salt and black pepper.

2 Combine the garlic, olive oil and lemon juice in an ovenproof dish. Add the sardines and turn to coat. Place in the fridge for 1 hour to marinate.

3 Place the marinated sardines in a preheated oven at 180°C and cook for 3–4 minutes per side, until the flesh turns opaque and flakes easily.

4 Squeeze over some lemon juice and season with sea salt and black pepper. Serve with extra lemon wedges, and garlic bread to mop up the juices.

Chef's tips

- To braai the sardines, remove them from the marinade and cook over prepared medium coals for 3–4 minutes per side, turning halfway.

Braaied Chilli Prawns

Prawns are great in any season, and there are so many ways to prepare them. Here's an easy braaied prawn dish for balmy summer nights. On page 64, you'll find a prawn curry that is perfect for cooler weather.

PREP TIME COOKING TIME SERVES

10 MINUTES

3–5 MINUTES

4

+ defrosting

1 kg queen prawns
2 Tbsp olive oil
Juice of 1–2 lemons
½ tsp ground paprika
½ tsp cayenne pepper
½ tsp garlic powder
½ tsp ground black pepper
1 cup finely chopped fresh dill
2 Tbsp butter
2 garlic cloves, crushed
   or thinly sliced
2 fresh green or red chillies,
   finely chopped
Wooden or metal skewers

1 Defrost the prawns according to the package instructions. Remove the heads, shells and central veins, but leave the tails on. Rinse the prawns and pat dry on paper towel.

2 Combine the olive oil, lemon juice, paprika, cayenne pepper, garlic powder, black pepper and chopped dill in a bowl. Add the prawns and toss to coat. Thread 4–5 prawns onto each skewer, ensuring they fit closely together (this will keep them moist and juicy).

3 Melt the butter in a small pan over medium heat. Add the fresh garlic and chillies and fry until the garlic is golden brown. Remove from the heat and keep warm.

4. Prepare the braai with medium coals. Place the prawn skewers on the grid and braai for 3 minutes, turning once, until the flesh turns opaque. Place the prawns on a serving platter, baste with the warm chilli-butter and serve immediately with hot garlic bread.

Prawn AND Peanut Curry

This creamy Thai-style curry is a great option for those autumn evenings when it is getting cooler, but you're not quite ready to say goodbye to summer.

PREP TIME

10 MINUTES

COOKING TIME

8-10 MINUTES

SERVES

4

+ defrosting

1 kg queen prawns
1 can (400 ml) coconut milk
1 Tbsp smooth peanut butter
1 Tbsp red curry paste
1 cinnamon stick
2–3 Tbsp lime juice
   or lemon juice
1 tsp fish sauce
1 tsp black pepper
½ tsp salt
Lime or lemon wedges,
   for serving

1. Defrost the prawns according to the package instructions. Remove the heads, shells and central veins, but leave the tails on. Rinse the prawns and pat dry on paper towel.

2. Heat the coconut milk in a large pan over medium heat until bubbles start to appear. Add the peanut butter and curry paste and stir to dissolve. Add the cinnamon stick and simmer for 2–3 minutes. Add the lime juice or lemon juice, fish sauce, and salt and pepper and cook for a further 2 minutes, until the sauce thickens slightly.

3. Add the prawns and cook for 3 minutes, until the flesh turns opaque. Check the seasoning and add more salt and/or pepper to taste. Serve with jasmine rice and stir-fried vegetables, with lime or lemon wedges on the side.

STREET FOOD AT HOME

CHICKEN FEAST

Chicken-on-the-go is normally sold by street vendors close to bus and taxi ranks or in busy areas in the township, where it is a popular snack or quick meal. To cook your own street feast at home, prepare a braai with medium-hot coals. (For a kettle braai, prepare the charcoal for direct cooking.) Remember that any marinade used on raw (uncooked) meat should be boiled for at least 5 minutes to destroy harmful bacteria before being used as a basting sauce for cooked meat. All the chicken feast recipes serve 4, but they can easily be doubled or trebled to cater for a crowd.

Chicken Heads

PREP TIME
10 MINUTES
+ 1 hour marinating time

COOKING TIME
10 MINUTES
over prepared coals

SERVES
4

12 clean chicken heads

MARINADE
½ cup (125 ml) BBQ sauce
2 Tbsp canola oil or
   sunflower oil
1 tsp ground paprika
1 tsp cayenne pepper
1 tsp garlic powder

1 Combine the marinade ingredients in a bowl. Add the chicken heads and turn to coat. Cover and leave in the fridge to marinate for 1 hour. Remove the heads from the marinade and boil the marinade for 5 minutes before using for basting.
2 Braai over medium coals for 10 minutes, turning and basting occasionally with the remaining marinade.

Chef's tip
• Instead of braaiing the chicken heads, place them in a roasting dish in the oven at 180ºC for 20–25 minutes, or pan-fry over medium heat for 15–20 minutes, turning frequently.

Chicken Feet

PREP TIME

10 MINUTES

+ 1 hour marinating time

COOKING TIME

20 MINUTES

over prepared coals

SERVES

4

20 clean chicken feet (± 1 kg)

MARINADE

½ cup (125 ml) chilli sauce
2 Tbsp canola oil or sunflower oil
1 tsp chilli powder
1 tsp ground paprika
1 tsp black pepper
½ tsp salt

1 Combine the marinade ingredients in a bowl. Add the chicken feet and turn to coat. Cover and leave in the fridge to marinate for 1 hour. Remove the feet from the marinade and boil the marinade for 5 minutes before using for basting, *see* Chef's tips.

2 Braai over medium coals for 20 minutes, turning occasionally, and basting with the remaining marinade.

Chef's tips

• Marinade used on raw (uncooked) meat should be boiled for at least 5 minutes, to destroy harmful bacteria, before being used as a basting sauce for cooked meat. Meat can be basted with uncooked marinade only during the first few minutes of cooking, as the heat of the fire will kill off any bacteria.

Gizzards

PREP TIME

10
MINUTES

+ 1 hour marinating time

COOKING TIME

30
MINUTES

over prepared coals.

SERVES

4

1 kg precooked gizzards, *see Chef's tips*

MARINADE

4 Tbsp soy sauce
4 Tbsp chilli sauce
2 garlic cloves, crushed or finely chopped
2 chillies, finely chopped
1 tsp cayenne pepper
1 tsp ground paprika

1 Combine the marinade ingredients in a bowl. Add the cooked gizzards and turn to coat. Cover and leave in the fridge to marinate for 1 hour. Remove the gizzards from the marinade and boil the marinade for 5 minutes before using for basting.

2 Soak 4 wooden skewers in water for 30 minutes. Thread 3–4 gizzards onto each skewer. Braai over medium coals for 30 minutes, turning frequently, and basting with the remaining marinade.

Chef's tips

• To precook gizzards, place them in a pot with water to cover and 1 tsp salt. Bring to the boil and cook for 30 minutes. Drain and pat dry. (If using frozen gizzards, defrost completely before cooking.) See also page 12.

Chicken Dust

'Chicken dust' is township-speak for a whole braaied chicken. 'Ama-pieces' refers to any chicken pieces. If you like, you can use an 8-piece braai pack – just don't call it 'chicken dust!'.

PREP TIME
10 MINUTES
+ 1 hour marinating time

COOKING TIME
50-75 MINUTES
over prepared coals

SERVES
4

1 whole chicken

MARINADE
½ cup (125 ml) BBQ sauce
4 Tbsp canola oil or sunflower oil
2 Tbsp lemon juice
1 Tbsp ground paprika
1 tsp ground cumin
1 tsp cayenne pepper
1 tsp chilli powder
1 tsp mustard powder
1 tsp garlic powder
1 tsp brown sugar
1 tsp black pepper
1 tsp salt

1. Combine the marinade ingredients in a bowl. Add the chicken and turn to coat. Cover and leave in the fridge for 1 hour. Remove the chicken from the marinade and boil the marinade for 5 minutes before using for basting.
2. Braai the chicken over medium coals for about 1 hour, until golden brown, turning frequently, and basting with the remaining marinade.

Chef's tips

- A whole chicken takes 1–1¼ hours to cook on a braai; a spatch-cocked chicken (flattie) takes 45–55 minutes; and chicken pieces take 30–40 minutes, depending on the cut (wings take less time than thighs).
- If using chicken pieces, put the thighs and drumsticks on the braai first, then add the breasts and wings after about 10 minutes. This will ensure that everything is ready at the same time.

MEATY FEAST

Serve this when friends come over to watch the beautiful game (or just to have a drink… or three). If you prepare the entire feast, you might discover a lot of new 'friends' who want to spend time at your place! All the recipes serve 4, depending on how hungry you are.

Shisanyama

[BRAAIED MEAT PLATTER]

PREP TIME	COOKING TIME	SERVES
10 MINUTES	**10–20** MINUTES	**4**
+ 1 hour marinating time	over prepared coals	

1 kg boerewors, twisted into links

1 kg beef short ribs

1 kg beef chuck, cut into strips

MARINADE

2 Tbsp (30 ml) canola oil or
   sunflower oil

2 Tbsp (30 ml) soy sauce

2 Tbsp brown sugar

1 Tbsp ground paprika

1 tsp dried origanum

1 tsp dried thyme

1 tsp salt

1 tsp black pepper

1 Combine the marinade ingredients in a large bowl. Add the meat and turn to coat. Cover and leave to marinate in the fridge for 1 hour. Remove the meat from the marinade and boil the marinade for at least 5 minutes before using for basting.

2 Braai over medium coals until done to your liking, turning frequently and basting with the remaining marinade. Serve with pap.

Chef's tips

• Allow the meat to come to room temperature before cooking. If you are using an open braai grid, make sure the pieces are big enough to not fall through. You don't want to ruin the feast by having to wipe ash off meat that has ended up on the coals!

• To ensure that everything will be ready at the same time, you need to braai the meat in the right sequence. Boerewors takes 15–18 minutes, ribs take 10–20 minutes, and the chuck strips will take 10–12 minutes.

Inyama Yenhloko

[BEEF LIP MEAT]

You'll find cleaned beef lip meat at township butchers and some fresh meat butchers in the suburbs.

PREP TIME	COOKING TIME	SERVES
10 MINUTES	2 HOURS	4

1 kg beef lip meat, cut into cubes

1 onion, chopped

3 garlic cloves, crushed
or finely chopped

4 cups (1 litre) boiling water

6 tsp beef stock powder

1 tsp salt

1 Tbsp black pepper

1 Place the lip meat, onion and garlic in a pot. Add the boiling water, stock powder and salt and pepper. Bring to a boil and cook for 2 hours. Remove from the pot and serve hot or cold.

Inqina Lenkomo
(COW'S TROTTERS)

The trotter is the lower part of the cow's leg, where it connects to the hoof.
It's made up of hardworking tendons that need long slow cooking
to convert them into succulent meat.

PREP TIME

20 MINUTES
+ marinating
time

COOKING TIME

2 HOURS
(in advance)

SERVES

4

1. Shred the meat from the bones, cutting up any larger pieces that can't be shredded, and place in a serving bowl. (You should end up with 3–4 cups of meat.)
2. Add the remaining ingredients and stir to combine. Cover the bowl with cling wrap and place in the fridge for 30–60 minutes, to marinate. Serve cold.

4 ready cooked trotters
2 Tbsp finely chopped garlic
2 Tbsp finely chopped chillies
  (green or red)
1 Tbsp sunflower oil or canola oil
1 tsp chilli powder
1 tsp cayenne pepper
1 tsp black pepper
½ tsp salt

Iskopo Semvu

[SHEEP'S HEAD]

You'll find sheep's heads (smileys) in township butchers and some butchers in the suburbs. To save time, buy a cooked head, or follow the instructions below for cleaning an uncooked head. Although this dish contains jalapeños, green chillies, chilli sauce and cayenne pepper, it is not as hot as it seems!

PREP TIME
20 MINUTES

COOKING TIME
2 HOURS
(in advance)

SERVES
4

1 cooked sheep's head,
  see Chef's tip
3 Tbsp bottled chilli sauce
2 Tbsp sliced fresh jalapeños
2 Tbsp finely chopped chillies
  (green or red)
10 garlic cloves, crushed
  or finely chopped
1 tsp cayenne pepper
1 tsp ground paprika

1 Shred the cooked meat from the bones, cutting up any pieces that can't be shredded, and place in a serving bowl. (You should end up with about 6 cups of meat.)
2 Add the chilli sauce, jalapeños, chillies, garlic, cayenne pepper and paprika and stir to combine. Serve cold, with hot pap.

Chef's tip

• To clean and prepare a sheep's head, cut off most of the hair, then burn off any remaining hair using a blowtorch or the flames from a fire. Scrub off the resulting blackness with a wire brush or scourer and rinse the head very well. Use an axe to chop the head in half, and clean the insides. Place the cleaned head in a large pot with salted water to cover, and boil for 2 hours, or until soft. Remove from the water and leave to cool before using as directed.

Bacon *and* Sausage Kota

The kota was born in Daveyton, a township in Ekhuruleni, on the East Rand. The name comes from urban slang for a 'quarter loaf'. This legendary township takeway is rivalled only by Durban's bunny chow and Cape Town's gatsby. Is there a winner? You'll have to take a very long road trip to try them all!

PREP TIME	COOKING TIME	MAKES
5 MINUTES	**10** MINUTES	**1** KOTA

Freshly made hot chips
3 bacon rashers
1 Russian sausage
1 Vienna sausage
1 thick polony slice
1 quarter white loaf, *see* Chef's tip
2 tsp mayonnaise
2 Tbsp atchaar
Rocket or lettuce leaves, optional
2–3 Tbsp grated cheese
Salt and black pepper to taste
Seasoning for chips to taste

TO PREPARE THE KOTA

Start by making the chips (*see* below). While the chips are cooking, pan-fry or deep-fry the bacon, Russian, Vienna and polony until warmed through. Remove the centre of the bread and set aside. Spread the mayonnaise in the hollow of the bread. Spoon over some atchaar, and add a few rocket or lettuce leaves, if preferred, followed by the cheese. Add a layer of hot chips, then the bacon rashers, sausages and polony. Replace the bread 'lid' and serve hot.

TO MAKE HOT CHIPS

Peel 1–2 medium potatoes per serving and cut into chips. Heat some sunflower oil or canola oil in a deep pot until bubbles start to form. Deep-fry the chips (do this in batches if necessary) until crisp and golden, then drain on kitchen paper to remove excess oil. Sprinkle with seasoning to taste.

Chef's tip

- Slice a loaf of bread in half lengthways, then divide each half into two, to get four kotas. (Unlike a bunny chow, which needs to be deep and 'bowl-shaped' to contain the curry sauce, the bread for a kota is shallower and 'boat-shaped'.)

Mince and Mash Kota

PREP TIME

15-20 MINUTES

COOKING TIME

25 MINUTES

MAKES

4 KOTAS

SAVOURY MINCE WITH MUSHROOMS

2 Tbsp canola oil or sunflower oil

1 medium onion, finely chopped

2 garlic cloves, crushed
or finely chopped

500 g beef mince

Salt and black pepper to taste

3–4 button mushrooms, chopped

3–4 Tbsp tomato paste

½ tsp cayenne pepper

½ tsp ground paprika

½ tsp beef stock powder mixed
with ¼ cup boiling water

MASHED POTATOES

3 large potatoes, peeled and
cut into chunks

1 Tbsp butter

½ cup (125 ml) milk

Salt and black pepper to taste

TO SERVE (PER KOTA)

1 quarter white loaf, *see* Chef's tip
on page 82

2 Tbsp atchaar

Grated cheese, optional

Fresh herbs or sprouts, optional

TO COOK THE MINCE AND MUSHROOMS

Heat the oil in a pan over medium heat. Add the onion and garlic and fry for 5 minutes. Add mince, salt and pepper and stir-fry for 2–3 minutes, until browned. Add the mushrooms, tomato paste and spices and continue to cook for 5 minutes. Add the stock and cook for 3–4 minutes more, until thickened. Keep warm.

TO COOK THE MASHED POTATOES

Boil the potato chunks in salted water until soft, about 10 minutes. Remove from the heat and drain. Return the potatoes to the pot whilst still hot, add the butter, and the milk bit by bit, mashing until smooth. Season to taste with salt and pepper and keep warm.

TO SERVE

Spoon a layer of mash into the kota. Drizzle over the atchaar then add some mince. Finish with the grated cheese and/or some fresh herbs. Replace the bread 'lid' and serve while hot.

Chef's tips

- Instead of beef stock, combine ½ tsp Bisto powder with ¼ cup boiling water.
- Reheat any leftover mince and mash in the microwave for a quick meal.

VEGETABLES

Spinach *and* Potatoes

PREP TIME
5–10 MINUTES

COOKING TIME
25 MINUTES

SERVES
4

2 Tbsp canola oil or sunflower oil

8–10 cups (400 g) chopped
spinach (chard)

2 Tbsp butter

1 onion, finely chopped

2 garlic cloves, crushed
or thinly sliced

2–3 medium potatoes (± 500 g),
peeled and cubed

2 tsp vegetable stock powder

500 ml boiling water

2 Tbsp plain cream cheese

Salt and black pepper to taste

1 Heat the oil in a pot and fry the spinach for 4–5 minutes,
until softened, then remove and set aside.

2 Heat the butter in the same pot and fry the onion and
garlic for about 2 minutes.

3 Add the cubed potatoes and fry for a further 5 minutes,
stirring occasionally, until golden.

4 Dissolve the stock powder in the boiling water and add
to the pot. Boil the potatoes until tender, about 10 minutes,
then drain off the water.

5 Return the spinach to the pot. Add the cream cheese and
salt and pepper to taste. Using a fork, mash the spinach
and potatoes together. Serve hot.

Chef's tips

- Ten cups of spinach may seem like a lot, but spinach shrinks as it
cooks. Allow about two heaped cups of uncooked chopped spinach
per serving.

- Imifino (morogo) is a general term for all leafy green vegetables,
whether home-grown, wild-harvested or commercially grown.

Muboora

Throughout the country, almost every vegetable patch has a pumpkin plant or two, making muboora (pumpkin leaves) an accessible source of leafy greens. Although they are not often eaten locally, pumpkin leaves are popular in both Zimbabwe and Mozambique.

PREP TIME
COOKING TIME
SERVES

500 ml water

1 tsp bicarbonate of soda

10 cups chopped muboora
(pumpkin leaves)

4 Tbsp sunflower oil or canola oil

1 red pepper, finely chopped

½ onion, finely chopped

2 garlic cloves, crushed
or very thinly sliced

1 tsp salt

2 tomatoes, chopped

1 Bring 500 ml water to boil in a large pot over high heat. Stir in the bicarbonate of soda, then add the chopped pumpkin leaves. Cover with a lid and boil for about 5 minutes, stirring occasionally, until just tender. Drain and set aside.

2 Reduce the heat to medium. Heat the oil in the same pot, then add the red pepper, onion, garlic and salt and cook for 2–3 minutes, until the onions and pepper have softened.

3 Add the tomatoes and cook for a further 2 minutes.

4 Return the pumpkin leaves and cook for 10–15 minutes, until the leaves are soft and the onions and tomatoes are cooked through.

Chef's tips

• Pumpkin leaves need to be prepared carefully, as they have small thorny spines along their length. Wash well to remove all traces of soil and dirt, then pull the leafy parts away from the central stem.

• Adding bicarb (bicarbonate of soda) to the cooking water helps to retain the natural bright green colour of leafy vegetables.

Moroho Wa Nkaka

Moroho is a Xitsonga collective term for leafy green vegetables
(also known as imifino, morogo and African spinach).
Moroho wa nkaka means 'moroho with peanuts'.

PREP TIME
10 MINUTES

COOKING TIME
25 MINUTES

SERVES
4

4 Tbsp sunflower oil or canola oil

1 onion, finely chopped

2 garlic cloves, crushed
   or finely chopped

200 g unsalted peanuts, crushed

20 g coconut flakes

2 tsp vegetable or chicken
   stock powder

400 ml boiling water

8–10 cups (± 400g) chopped
   moroho or chard spinach

Salt and black pepper to taste

1 Heat the oil in a pot on medium-high and fry the onion
   and garlic for 2 minutes, until just golden.
2 Add the peanuts and coconut flakes.
3 Dissolve the stock powder in the boiling water and add
   to the pot. Simmer for about 20 minutes, stirring
   occasionally, until the onions have softened and the liquid
   has reduced by half.
4 Meanwhile, place the moroho in a separate pot. Cover with
   water, and bring to a boil. Cook until tender (± 5 minutes),
   then drain.
5 Add the drained moroho to the onion-peanut mixture
   and stir to combine. Season to taste and serve hot as
   a vegetable side dish.

Spicy Spinach
WITH TOMATO AND ONION

PREP TIME
5 MINUTES

COOKING TIME
15 MINUTES

SERVES
4

3 Tbsp canola oil or sunflower oil

8–10 cups (400 g) chopped
 spinach (chard)

1 onion, finely chopped

2 garlic cloves, crushed
 or thinly sliced

1 Tbsp tomato paste

1 tsp ground paprika

1 tsp cayenne pepper

1 can (400 g) chopped tomatoes

Salt and black pepper to taste

1 Heat 2 Tbsp oil in a pot. Fry the spinach for 4–5 minutes, until softened, then remove and set aside.

2 Add the remaining oil to the pot, along with the onion and garlic and fry for 2 minutes, until the onion has softened.

3 Add the tomato paste, paprika and cayenne pepper and stir through. Add the chopped tomatoes and simmer for about 5 minutes.

4 Return the spinach to the pot and fold into the tomato and onion mixture. Season to taste and serve hot.

Imbuya

Imbuya, or amaranth (also known as Chinese spinach), grows in the wild in the Eastern Cape and adjacent areas, but you may struggle to find it in other parts of the country. The broad, green leaves can be eaten raw in salads, added to stir-fries, soups or stews, or even fermented, like kimchi.

PREP TIME 5 MINUTES

COOKING TIME 10 MINUTES

SERVES 4

2 Tbsp canola oil or sunflower oil

1 onion, finely chopped

2 garlic cloves, crushed
  or finely chopped

15 cups (± 600 g) chopped
  imbuya leaves

1 tsp vegetable or chicken
  stock powder

100 ml boiling water

Salt and black pepper to taste

1 Heat the oil in a pan on medium-high and fry the onion and garlic for about 2 minutes, until softened.

2 Add the imbuya leaves and stir-fry for 1 minute.

3 Combine the stock powder and boiling water and add to the pot. Continue cooking, stirring occasionally, until the stock has evaporated and the vegetables are tender, about 8 minutes. Season to taste and serve hot.

Mashed Potatoes
WITH GREEN BEANS AND MUSHROOMS

PREP TIME
10 MINUTES

COOKING TIME
20 MINUTES

SERVES
4

2-3 medium potatoes, peeled
and roughly chopped

2 Tbsp butter

1 onion, finely chopped

3 garlic cloves, crushed
or finely chopped

300 g green beans, chopped

250 g button mushrooms, sliced

1 tsp vegetable or chicken
stock powder

250 ml boiling water

2 Tbsp plain cream cheese

Salt and black pepper to taste

1 Place the potatoes in a pot and cover with water.
Boil until tender, about 10 minutes, then drain, place
in a mixing bowl and set aside.

2 Meanwhile, melt the butter in a pan. Add the onion
and garlic and fry for about 2 minutes, until softened.

3 Add the green beans and cook, stirring, until tender,
about 3-5 minutes.

4 Add the mushrooms and cook, stirring occasionally,
for a futher 3-5 minutes.

5 Crush the potatoes slightly, then add the bean and
mushroom mixture, stirring to combine. Season to taste
with salt and pepper.

6 Dissolve the stock powder in the boiling water and add
gradually to the vegetables, mashing them together to
your preferred texture. Stir in the cream cheese. Check
the seasoning and adjust if necessary.

Spicy Split Green Peas
WITH CHORIZO

I created this one day when I was playing around with different ingredients, and wondering what to do with them. Served with garlic bread, hot from the oven, it makes great comfort food on a cool winter's night.

PREP TIME
10 MINUTES
+ overnight soaking

COOKING TIME
60 MINUTES

SERVES
4

500 g split green peas, soaked overnight (ot at least 6 hours)
4 Tbsp olive oil
1 onion, finely chopped
3 garlic cloves, crushed or finely chopped
1 Tbsp finely chopped fresh ginger
2 jalapeño chillies or green chillies, finely chopped
Salt and ground black pepper to taste
250 g chorizo, cubed
1 tsp tomato paste
1 tsp cayenne pepper
1 tsp ground paprika
2 tomatoes, grated, or 1 can (400 g) chopped tomatoes
2 tsp vegetable or chicken stock powder dissolved in 500 ml boiling water
Fresh coriander, for serving

1 Drain the soaked peas, rinse and drain again. Place in a pot with water to cover. Bring to the boil, skimming off any foam, and cook for about 30 minutes, until soft 'to the tooth'. (If necessary, top up the pot with a little more boiling water.) Reserve 1 cup of the cooking water, then drain the peas and set aside.

2 Heat the oil in the same pot or a large pan. Fry the onion, garlic, ginger and chillies for about 3 minutes, until softened. Season to taste with salt and black pepper.

3 Add the chorizo and fry for a further 5 minutes.

4 Add the tomato paste and spices. Stir through and fry for another minute.

5 Return the drained peas to the pot, along with the tomatoes and stock. Cook on medium heat for 15–20 minutes, until the liquid has reduced and the peas have a thick, creamy consistency. (If necessary, add a little of the reserved cooking liquid.) Season to taste and serve hot in bowls. Eat with a spoon.

Corned Tongue

AND CHICKPEA SALAD

This main dish salad is ideal for a casual weekend meal, with some crusty bread on the side. It also makes a good packed lunch for work.

PREP TIME

5–10 MINUTES

SERVES

4

with precooked tongue

2 cans (400 g each) chickpeas
600 g corned tongue, sliced
200 g cherry tomatoes, halved
½ English cucumber, cubed
1 red onion, thinly sliced
1 cup fresh parsley, chopped
Salt and black pepper to taste
2 feta rounds, cubed
4 Tbsp extra-virgin olive oil
1–2 Tbsp lemon juice

1 Drain the chickpeas, rinse under running water and drain again.
2 Combine the chickpeas, tongue, tomatoes, cucumber, onion and most of the parsley in a serving bowl. Season to taste and toss gently to mix.
3 Add the feta, drizzle with olive oil and lemon juice, and scatter over the reserved parsley. Serve immediately, or cover and place in the fridge until required.

Chef's tips

• Buy an uncooked corned tongue and follow the cooking instructions on the package. Leave to cool then slice thinly or cut into cubes. Any tongue not used for the salad can be used for sandwiches.

• Instead of tongue, you can use pastrami, spiced beef, frankfurters or bockwurst.

Chilli Beans

PREP TIME

10 MINUTES

COOKING TIME

2 HOURS

SERVES

4

+ overnight soaking

1 kg dried red speckled beans
(pinto beans)

3 Tbsp olive oil

1 onion, finely chopped

1 red pepper, chopped

5 garlic cloves, finely chopped

2 red chillies, seeds removed
and finely chopped

1 jalapeño chilli, seeds removed
and finely chopped

1 habanero chilli, seeds removed
and finely chopped

1 celery stick, chopped

5–6 sprigs of fresh thyme

Salt and pepper to taste

1 Tbsp beef or chicken stock
powder dissolved in 1 litre
boiling water

1 Soak the beans overnight, then drain and rinse. Set aside.
2 Heat the olive oil in a pot and add the onion, red pepper,
   garlic, chillies, celery and thyme. Cook over a low heat for
   about 5 minutes until the onion and red pepper are soft and
   the chillies have released their flavours. Season to taste
   with salt and black pepper.
3 Add the beans to the pot and stir through.
4 Add the stock and stir to combine. Put a lid on the pot
   and simmer on a low heat for 1½–2 hours, until the beans
   are tender and creamy. (Stir periodically, and make sure the
   liquid doesn't boil away before the beans are tender; add
   a little more hot water if necessary.)
5 Season to taste, and serve in bowls with rice, or with
   some crusty bread on the side.

Chef's tip

• Jalapeño and 'Serenade' chillies are mild to medium heat, but
  habanero chillies, also known as Scotch bonnet, are very hot,
  as are green finger chillies. If you can't get a variety of chillies,
  use 3–4 chillies of your choice, according to your heat preference.

Meaty Brown Lentil Soup

PREP TIME

5 MINUTES

COOKING TIME

30 MINUTES

SERVES

4

3–4 Tbsp olive oil
1 onion, finely chopped
3 garlic cloves, crushed
   or thinly sliced
1 celery stalk, chopped
1 carrot, chopped
250 g beef mince
1 Tbsp tomato paste
1 tsp ground paprika
1 tsp BBQ spice
2 cups (± 250 g) dried brown lentils,
   rinsed and drained
3 Tbsp beef stock powder dissolved
   in 2 litres boiling water
2 tomatoes, chopped, or
   1 can (400 g) chopped tomatoes
2 dried bay leaves
Salt and pepper to taste

1 Heat the oil in a pot and fry the onion, garlic, celery and carrot until just softened.
2 Add the mince and fry for 4–5 minutes, until browned.
3 Stir in the tomato paste and spices and cook for 1 minute until incorporated.
4 Add the lentils, hot stock, chopped tomatoes, bay leaves and salt and pepper to taste. Bring to the boil then lower the heat to medium and cook for 20–30 minutes, until the lentils are soft.
5 Remove the bay leaves. Using a hand-held blender, pulse the soup a few times to blend the ingredients. (Don't make it too smooth, you want to retain some texture.) Check the seasoning and adjust if necessary. Serve with slices of crusty bread or seed loaf.

Homemade Baked Beans
WITH A TWIST

Most baked beans are made in the oven, but this recipe cooks them on the stove. Although they are 'simmered' rather than 'baked', that doesn't mean they aren't just as tasty! Serve hot as a vegetable dish or cold as a side salad.

PREP TIME
10 MINUTES
+ overnight soaking

COOKING TIME
80 MINUTES

SERVES
4

2 cups (± 500 g) dried haricot beans, soaked, *see* Chef's tips
Canola oil or sunflower oil, for frying
1 onion, finely chopped
3 garlic cloves, crushed or thinly sliced
1 tsp garlic powder
1 tsp onion powder
1 tsp black pepper
½ tsp salt
1 Tbsp tomato paste
3 tsp chicken stock powder dissolved in 750 ml boiling water
½ cup (125 ml) tomato sauce
3 Tbsp honey
1 Tbsp lemon juice
1 Tbsp minestrone soup powder

1 Place the drained beans in a pot with water to cover and simmer over low to medium heat for 50–60 minutes, until soft but not mushy. Drain.

2 Heat a little oil in a pot. Add the onion and garlic and fry until softened.

3 Stir in the spices and tomato paste and cook for 1 minute, then add the remaining ingredients, except the soup powder, and stir through.

4 Add the cooked beans and simmer for about 10 minutes, stirring occasionally, until they are soft and the liquid has reduced.

5 Combine the minestrone soup powder with 2–3 Tbsp warm water to make a paste and add to the beans. Stir through and continue cooking for 5 minutes, until thickened.

Chef's tips

• To prepare the dried beans, place in a bowl with water to cover and soak overnight, or for at least 6 hours. Drain and rinse.

• Haricot beans, also known as white beans or Boston beans, are traditionally used for baked beans, both homemade and canned.

GOGO'S RECIPES

Isijingi

Isijngi is a warm butternut and maize meal porridge
(some call it pudding) that can be enjoyed at any time of the day or night.

PREP TIME
5 MINUTES

COOKING TIME
30 MINUTES

SERVES
4

2 cups cubed butternut
2–3 cups (500–750 ml) water
1 cup maize meal
½ cup brown sugar
Toasted pumpkin seeds,
    optional, for garnish

1 Place the butternut in a pot with just enough water to cover and cook over medium heat until most of the water has cooked away and the butternut is tender. Mash the butternut until smooth.

2 In a bowl, combine the maize meal with 1 cup water, stirring to make a paste.

3 Add the maize meal paste to mashed butternut in the pot. Stir to combine and cook over medium heat, stirring, for 15–20 minutes, until the mixture thickens. Add a little extra water if it seems too dry.

4 Stir in the sugar and continue simmering for a further 5 minutes. To add some crunch, scatter over toasted pumpkin seeds before serving.

Chef's tips

- For a flavour booster, add some butter just before serving.
- Isijingi is just as delicious when made with pumpkin.

Amathambo
MARROW BONES WITH PASTA

This hearty dish is perfect for cold nights.

PREP TIME

10 MINUTES

COOKING TIME

75 MINUTES

SERVES
4

1 kg beef marrow bones
1 onion, roughly chopped
5 garlic cloves, chopped
2 bay leaves
2–3 sprigs fresh thyme
2–3 tsp beef stock powder
1 litre (4 cups) boiling water
1 cup elbow macaroni
2 Tbsp oxtail soup powder

1 Rinse the bones and place them in a large pot with the onion, garlic, bay leaves and thyme.
2 Dissolve the beef stock powder in the boiling water and add to the pot. Simmer over medium heat for 1 hour, until the meat is tender and starting to fall off the bone. (Top up with a little extra boiling water if necessary.)
3 While the meat is cooking, cook the macaroni according to the package instructions, then drain and set aside.
4 When the meat is ready, stir in the macaroni and cook for 5 minutes.
5 Combine the oxtail soup powder with just enough warm water to make a paste and add to the pot. Cook for a further 5 minutes to thicken the stew.

Creamy Mushroom
MAIZE RICE

Serve this with meat dishes instead of traditional rice.

PREP TIME
10 MINUTES

COOKING TIME
70 MINUTES

SERVES
4

1 cup maize rice

2 cups (500 ml) water

Salt and ground black pepper
  to taste

2 Tbsp butter

1 onion, finely chopped

5 garlic cloves, crushed
  or very finely chopped

250 g button mushrooms,
  thinly sliced

½ cup (125 ml) cream

1 Rinse and drain the maize rice. Bring the water to a boil
   in a pot. Add the maize rice and salt to taste. Cover with
   a lid, lower the heat and simmer for 40–60 minutes, stirring
   occasionally, until the water has evaporated and the maize
   rice is tender. (It will be slightly sticky when cooked, not
   fluffy and light.)

2 Meanwhile, melt the butter in a pan and fry the onion
   and garlic for 2–3 minutes, until soft.

3 Add the mushrooms and cook until softened, about
   10 minutes. Season to taste with salt and pepper.

4 When the maize rice is ready, add the onion and mushroom
   mix to the pot and stir through. Stir in the cream and adjust
   the seasoning, if necessary.

Steamed Mealie Bread

This is traditionally made by wrapping the dough in mealie husks.
Whole mealie cobs with husks are not always available in supermarkets,
so if you can't get 'leafy mealies', wrap the dough in foil instead.

PREP TIME
15 MINUTES

COOKING TIME
40 MINUTES

MAKES
4
individual breads

4–6 sweetcorn or mealie cobs
  with husks, or 6 cups sweetcorn
  kernels (fresh or frozen)
½ cup (125 ml) sugar
2 Tbsp butter or margarine, melted
2 Tbsp self-raising flour

1 Cut the kernels off the cobs into a mixing bowl (you need about 6 cups). Wash the husks and set them aside for wrapping the bread. Mash the kernels with a wooden spoon or fork until very smooth.

2 Add the sugar, melted butter or margarine and self-raising flour and mix to a dough-like consistency. Knead the dough in the bowl until combined, about 10 minutes.

3 Divide the dough into four pieces and wrap each piece in a mealie husk, folding it around the dough to enclose it. (You may need to soak the husks in a little hot water to soften them.)

4 Put the parcels in a colander placed over a pot of boiling water, cover with a lid, and steam for 30–40 minutes. They are done when a skewer poked into the centre of the dough comes out clean. Remove from the steamer and place on a wire rack to cool before serving.

Steamed Bread

Dombolo, or steamed bread, is often stuffed with tasty fillings,
like mince and cabbage. Instead of making one large loaf for sharing,
you can make individual breads in enamel mugs.

DOMBOLO (STEAMED BREAD)

PREP TIME	STEAMING TIME	MAKES
50 MINUTES	**45** MINUTES	**1** LOAF
including rising time		serves 6–8

6 cups (6 × 250 ml) flour, plus extra
    for dusting

1 sachet (10 g) instant dry yeast

3 Tbsp sugar

1 tsp salt

1 litre warm water

2 Tbsp butter, for greasing

1 Place the flour, yeast, sugar and salt into a bowl. Make a well in the centre and add the water bit by bit, stirring to combine into a smooth dough, then knead for 5 minutes until it is smooth and elastic. Cover the dough with a clean cloth or cling wrap and set aside in a warm place for 20 minutes, until doubled in size. (While you wait, make the mince and cabbage stuffing.)

2 When the dough has risen, knock it back, then form into a ball, cover with a clean cloth and set aside for 5 minutes to rise again.

3 Dust your work surface with flour. Turn out the dough and press into a round shape. Pile the cooled mince and cabbage stuffing into the centre of the dough, and fold over the edges to fully enclose the stuffing. Carefully place the dough in an enamel bowl that has been greased with butter. (For individual breads, divide the dough and filling into 8 portions, and make small dough parcels that will fit into greased enamel mugs.)

4 Place the bowl or mugs inside a pot and carefully pour in enough boiling water to reach halfway up the sides. Cover with a tight-fitting lid and steam on medium heat for 45 minutes, or until the bread is cooked through and the filling is hot. (A skewer inserted into the centre of the loaf should come out clean and be hot to the touch.)

5 Remove the cooked bread from the bowl and leave to cool slightly before cutting into thick wedges to serve.

MINCE AND CABBAGE STUFFING

PREP TIME

COOKING TIME

4 Tbsp canola oil or sunflower oil

3–4 Tbsp finely chopped onion

3 garlic cloves, crushed
    or very finely chopped

500 g beef mince

1 tsp ground paprika

Salt and black pepper to taste

1 Tbsp Bisto gravy powder

1 cup (250 ml) boiling water

5 cups finely chopped cabbage

1 While the dough is rising, heat the oil in a pan over medium heat and fry the onion and garlic for 2–3 minutes.

2 Add the mince, paprika and salt and pepper to taste.

3 Combine the Bisto with the boiling water and add to the mince. Fry, stirring occasionally, for 5–10 minutes, until the onions are golden and the mince is cooked through.

4 Add the cabbage and fry for a further 2 minutes, until wilted. Set aside to cool. (The filling needs to be cool when you stuff the dough.)

Spinach Pap

PREP TIME

10 MINUTES

COOKING TIME

20 MINUTES

SERVES

4

2 Tbsp butter
1 onion, finely chopped
5 garlic cloves, crushed
  or finely chopped
4 cups finely chopped spinach
Salt and black pepper to taste
2 cups (500 ml) boiling water
1 kg maize meal

1 Melt the butter in a pot. Add the onion and garlic and cook over medium heat for about 5 minutes, until softened.

2 Add the spinach and stir through. Season to taste with salt and pepper.

3 Add the boiling water and gradually pour in the maize meal, whisking constantly for about 5 minutes, until you have a smooth consistency. Put a lid on the pot, lower the heat and leave to steam for about 10 minutes.

Fried Chicken

This is my take on everyone's favourite American fried chicken.
The chicken is fried first, and then baked, which makes it deliciously crispy.
This recipe makes one serving; to feed the family (or a crowd!),
just multiply the ingredients by the number of servings.

PREP TIME

10 MINUTES
+ soaking time

FRYING TIME

10 MINUTES
+ 5 minutes baking time

SERVES

1

3 chicken pieces (thighs and/or drumsticks are best)
3 large eggs
½ cup (125 ml) milk
2 tsp mustard powder
1 tsp chicken spice
1 tsp dried parsley
1 tsp dried thyme
1 tsp black pepper
Pinch of salt
1½ cups flour
Canola oil or sunflower oil for frying

1 Using a sharp knife, make a few small cuts in the chicken, to allow the flavours to penetrate.
2 Combine the eggs and milk in a bowl and beat lightly. Add the seasonings and stir through.
3 Place the chicken pieces in the egg mixture, turning until well coated, and place in the fridge overnight (or for at least 1 hour).
4 When ready to cook, remove the chicken from the egg mixture and place on a wire rack to drain. Place the flour in a bowl with some salt and pepper and add the chicken pieces, tossing until well coated.
5 Heat the oil in a pan over high heat and fry the chicken until golden brown on all sides (6–10 minutes), then drain on kitchen towel. (If you are cooking more than three pieces, fry them in batches because if you overcrowd the pan, the temperature of the oil will drop too much and the chicken won't get crisp.)
6 Place the fried chicken on a baking sheet in a preheated oven at 200°C for 15 minutes, until cooked through.

Chef's tip

• Preparing the chicken in advance and leaving it in the batter for a few hours, or overnight, allows the flavours to penetrate the meat, giving it that spicy juiciness we all crave.

Amagwinya

These fried dough balls, also called vetkoek, are great for breakfast, with savoury toppings. Instead of the balls, I make mine into squares. To save time on busy mornings, make them ahead and reheat in the microwave.

PREP TIME
35 MINUTES
(including rising time)

COOKING TIME
5 MINUTES

SERVES
4

6 cups (6 × 250 ml) flour
3 Tbsp sugar
1 sachet (10 g) instant dry yeast
1 tsp salt
1 litre (4 cups) warm water
Canola oil or sunflower oil, for deep frying
Sliced polony, for serving
Atchar or chutney, for serving
Grated cheese, for serving

1 Combine the dry ingredients in a bowl. Add the water, bit by bit, and mix to a dough-like consistency.

2 Knead the dough in the bowl for about 10 minutes, until it is smooth and no longer sticky. Shape into a ball, cover the bowl with a clean cloth, and leave to rise in a warm place for about 20 minutes, until it doubles in size.

3 Knock back the risen dough. Turn out onto a lightly floured surface and use your hands to shape it into a rough square. Using a sharp knife, cut the dough into squares, about 4 × 4 cm in size.

4 Heat the oil in a large pot on medium heat until bubbles start to form. Deep-fry the amagwinya in batches, turning them until they are golden brown on all sides (3–4 minutes), then drain on kitchen paper. Serve hot, with some polony, atchar and grated cheese, and a cup of tea on the side.

Creamy Samp

Serve with meat and/or vegetables for a wholesome family meal.

 PREP TIME **10** MINUTES

 COOKING TIME **1½** HOURS

 SERVES **4**

+ soaking time

1 kg dried samp
6 cups (1½ litres) water
4 Tbsp butter
5–6 spring onions, finely chopped
5 garlic cloves, crushed
  or finely chopped
½ cup grated mozzarella
  or Parmesan-style cheese
½ cup (125 ml) cream
Salt and ground black pepper
  to taste
2 Tbsp mushroom soup powder
½ cup (125 ml) boiling water

1 Rinse and drain the samp. Place in a bowl with cold water to cover and leave to soak for at least 8 hours, or overnight, then drain and rinse again.

2 Place the drained samp and water in a large pot. Bring to the boil, then lower the heat and simmer over low heat for 60–80 minutes, stirring occasionally, until tender. If necessary, top up with a little extra water.

3 While the samp is cooking, melt the butter in a large pot. Add the spring onions and garlic and cook for a few minutes, to soften.

4 Add the cooked samp to the pot and stir in the grated cheese and cream. Season to taste with salt and pepper. Simmer, stirring occasionally, for 10 minutes until the samp is smooth and creamy.

5 Combine the mushroom soup powder with the boiling water to make a smooth paste. Stir into the samp and continue cooking for another 5 minutes. Adjust the consistency according to your preference by adding a little extra water, milk or cream. Serve hot.

Samp *and* Beans
WITH POTATOES

The addition of potatoes adds a twist to this traditional favourite.

PREP TIME
10 MINUTES

COOKING TIME
2 HOURS

SERVES
4

+ soaking time

1 kg dried samp
250 g dried speckled (sugar) beans
500 g potatoes, peeled and
   quartered
1 onion, finely chopped
5 garlic cloves, crushed
   or finely chopped
6–8 cups (1½–2 litres) water
2 Tbsp chicken or vegetable
   stock powder
2 dried bay leaves
Salt and ground black pepper
   to taste

1 Rinse and drain the samp and beans. Combine in a large bowl with cold water to cover and leave to soak for at least 8 hours, or overnight, then drain and rinse again.

2 Place the drained samp and beans, potatoes, onion, garlic and water in a large pot. Add the stock powder, bay leaves and salt and pepper to taste.

3 Bring to the boil, then lower the heat and simmer over low heat for 1½–2 hours, stirring occasionally, until tender. If necessary, top up with a little extra water.

4 Before serving, stir with a fork to break up the potatoes, remove the bay leaves and adjust the seasoning to taste.

Mzansi Jollof Rice

In West Africa, jollof often includes meat cooked in the pot along with the rice. As this is a meat-free version, it makes a great accompaniment to meat or vegetables. Your choice of chillies will determine how hot the finished dish is. Are you going to play it safe, or go for the burn?

PREP TIME
10 MINUTES

COOKING TIME
25–30 MINUTES

SERVES
6

2 Tbsp olive oil

2 red peppers, finely chopped

1 onion, finely chopped

2 tomatoes, chopped

3 garlic cloves, crushed
  or very finely chopped

1–2 tsp finely chopped
  fresh chillies

2 tsp ground paprika

1 tsp cayenne pepper

1 tsp dried thyme

4 dried bay leaves

Salt and ground black pepper
  to taste

2–3 Tbsp tomato paste

6 tsp chicken stock powder

3 cups (750 ml) boiling water

2 cups (400 g) basmati rice

1 Heat the oil in a large pot over medium heat. Add the red peppers and onion and fry for 2–3 minutes, until soft.

2 Add the tomatoes, garlic, chilli, paprika, cayenne pepper, dried thyme, dried bay leaves and salt and pepper to taste. Cook for 10 minutes, stirring frequently. Stir in the tomato paste and cook for another minute.

3 Combine the stock powder with the boiling water and stir into the pot. Increase the heat to high. Add the rice and cook for 10–15 minutes, until the liquid has evaporated and the rice is tender.

Chef's tip

• Habanero and Scotch bonnet are two varieties of hot chillies that are traditionally used for jollof. If you prefer a milder dish, opt for medium-hot serrano (Serenade) chillies or milder jalapeños.

Lime Couscous

Serve this, hot or cold, with grilled or braaied chicken, fish or meat.

PREP TIME **5** MINUTES

COOKING TIME **15** MINUTES

SERVES **4**

100 ml olive oil
½ onion, finely chopped
5 garlic cloves, crushed
  or very finely chopped
4 tsp chicken stock powder
2 cups (500 ml) boiling water
Juice and zest of 1–2 limes
Salt and black pepper to taste
2 cups (2 × 250 ml) couscous
Fresh basil

1 Heat the oil in a pot over medium heat and fry the onion and garlic for 3–4 minutes, until soft.

2 Combine the stock powder with the boiling water. Add to the pot, along with the lime juice and zest, and salt and pepper to taste. Bring to the boil, then remove from the heat and stir in the couscous. Put a lid on the pot and leave to stand for 5 minutes, to allow the couscous to swell and absorb the flavours. Fluff the couscous with a fork, tip into a serving bowl, and garnish with fresh basil.

Lemon *and* Herb Rice

PREP TIME

10 MINUTES

COOKING TIME

20 MINUTES

SERVES

8

3 cups Tastic Long Grain
   Parboiled Rice
1 cup finely chopped chives
1 cup finely chopped parsley
½ cup finely chopped mint
½ cup finely chopped coriander
½ cup (125 ml) olive oil
2–3 Tbsp lemon juice
1 cup finely grated Parmesan
   or hard cheese
1 tsp truffle oil, optional

1 Bring 5–6 cups (± 1½ litres) water and 2 tsp salt to the
   boil. Add the rice, lower the heat and simmer, uncovered,
   for 10–15 minutes. Drain any excess water and rinse under
   cold running water.
2 Transfer the cooled rice to a serving bowl. Add the rest of
   the ingredients and mix well. Serve with your choice
   of meat.

See page 128

Vegetable Brown Rice

PREP TIME
10 MINUTES

COOKING TIME
45 MINUTES

SERVES
6

2 cups Tastic Wholegrain
   Long Grain Brown Rice
4 Tbsp olive oil
1 medium onion, finely chopped
4 garlic cloves, crushed or very
   finely chopped
1 red pepper, finely chopped
1 cup sweetcorn
1 cup green beans,
   finely chopped
1 cup carrots, finely chopped
1 cup spring onions,
   finely chopped
Salt and ground black pepper
   to taste

1 Place the rice in a large pot. Add 5–6 cups (± 1½ litres) water and 2–3 tsp salt and bring to the boil, then reduce the heat, cover, and simmer for 35–40 minutes, until all the water has been absorbed.

2 While the rice is cooking, heat the olive oil in a pan. Add the onion and garlic and fry until aromatic and soft. Add the vegetables and stir-fry for 10 minutes, until the vegetables are tender but still crunchy. Season to taste with salt and pepper.

3 Add the vegetables to the rice and stir through. Serve hot or cold.

Chef's tip

• Instead of fresh vegetables, use a 500 g packet of mixed frozen vegetables.

See page 129

Curried Rice

PREP TIME
5 MINUTES

COOKING TIME
20 MINUTES

SERVES
6

4 Tbsp olive oil
1 large onion, finely chopped
3 garlic cloves, crushed or finely
  chopped
1 Tbsp curry powder
1 tsp ground turmeric
2–3 Tbsp dried curry leaves
2 dried bay leaves
1 tsp salt
1 tsp black pepper
2 cups (500 ml) vegetable or
  chicken stock
2 cups Tastic Rices of the World
  Basmati Rice

1 Heat the oil in a large pot. Add the onion and garlic and fry until translucent and aromatic.
2 Add the curry powder, turmeric, dried curry leaves, dried bay leaves and salt and pepper and cook for a further two minutes.
3 Add the stock and bring to the boil, then add the rice and cook for 12–15 minutes, until the water is absorbed and the rice is soft. Serve with your choice of meat.

See page 128

Rainbow Rice Salad

PREP TIME

20 MINUTES

COOKING TIME

45 MINUTES

SERVES

6

2 cups Tastic Brown & Wild Rice
1 cup halved cherry tomatoes
5 hardboiled eggs, halved
1 cup feta, cubed
1 cup sliced red onion
1 cup black olives

DRESSING
½ cup (125 ml) olive oil
4–6 Tbsp lemon juice
1 Tbsp dried origanum
1 Tbsp finely chopped garlic
1 tsp salt
1 tsp black pepper

1 Place the rice in a large pot. Add 5–6 cups (± 1½ litres) water and 2–3 tsp salt and bring to the boil, then reduce the heat, cover, and simmer for 35–40 minutes, until all the water has been absorbed. Set aside until cool.

2 While the salad is cooling, combine all the dressing ingredients in a jug or bowl and set aside.

3 To make the salad, spread the rice on a large platter and arrange the ingredients in rows across the top. Drizzle over the dressing.

SALADS

Green Salad

I grew up with this simple salad, dressed with vinegar and olive oil.
It's still one of my favourites.

PREP TIME
20 MINUTES

SERVES
4

1. Whisk the dressing ingredients together in a small jug or bowl and set aside.
2. Arrange the salad ingredients in a serving bowl or on a platter. Pour over the dressing and toss lightly.

1 iceberg lettuce, or packet of mixed leaves, shredded
½ cucumber, cut into half moons
2–3 medium tomatoes, sliced
1 red onion, thinly sliced
2 rounds of feta, cubed
1 cup black olives

BASIC VINAIGRETTE

½ cup (125 ml) olive oil
½ cup (125 ml) balsamic vinegar or apple cider vinegar
3 garlic cloves, crushed or finely chopped
1 Tbsp lemon juice
Salt and black pepper to taste

Salsa

The secret to salsa is to chop everything to the same size,
so nothing dominates and you get a taste of everything with each bite.

PREP TIME
10–15
MINUTES

SERVES
4

1 Combine all the ingredients in a serving bowl.
Place in the fridge to chill before serving.

2 tomatoes, finely chopped

½–1 cucumber, finely chopped

1 medium onion, finely chopped

1 cup finely chopped dill pickles

1 cup finely chopped fresh basil

1 cup finely chopped fresh
   coriander

5 garlic cloves, finely chopped

½ cup (125 ml) olive oil

½ cup (125 ml) apple cider vinegar

2 Tbsp lemon juice

Salt and black pepper to taste

Rocket *and* Halloumi
SALAD

PREP TIME

SERVES

4 cups rocket (± 160 g)
2–3 medium tomatoes, quartered
1 red onion, thinly sliced
1 cup olives
± 300 g pan-fried halloumi cheese,
   see Chef's tip

OLIVE OIL & MUSTARD DRESSING

½ cup (125 ml) olive oil
1 Tbsp Dijon mustard
½ cup finely chopped chives
½ cup finely chopped parsley
Salt and black pepper to taste

1 Combine the rocket, tomatoes, onion and olives on
   a serving platter.
2 Top with the warm halloumi.
3 Pour over the dressing and serve immediately.

FOR THE DRESSING

1 Whisk the dressing ingredients together in a jug
   or small bowl.

Chef's tip

• To pan-fry halloumi, cut it into fingers, about ½-cm thick and pat dry.
Spray a nonstick grill pan with cooking spray and preheat. Fry the
halloumi in the hot pan for 1–2 minutes on each side, until golden.
Drain on paper towel.

Carrot *and* Bean Salad
WITH PEPPADEWS

Peppadews®, also known as sweet chilli peppers or piquanté peppers, add a bit of heat to this salad.

 PREP TIME 10 MINUTES

 COOKING TIME 15 MINUTES

 SERVES 4

3–4 medium carrots, cut into strips or julienned, *see* Chef's tip

2 cups (± 200 g) green beans, halved lengthways

2 Tbsp olive oil

1 red onion, very thinly sliced

3 garlic cloves, crushed or finely chopped

1 Tbsp BBQ spice

1 can (400 g) red kidney beans, drained and rinsed

½ cup Peppadews®, drained and roughly chopped

½ cup parsley or microherbs, plus extra for garnish

1 Place the carrots in a pot with water to cover. Bring to the boil for 10 minutes, then add the green beans and cook for a further 3 minutes. Drain and set aside to cool.

2 Heat the oil in a pan. Add the onion, garlic and BBQ spice and fry until golden and tender, about 4 minutes.

3 Combine the cooked carrots, beans and onion mixture in a serving bowl.

4 Add the kidney beans, Peppadews® and chopped parsley or microherbs and toss lightly. Chill in the fridge, and garnish with extra parsley or microherbs before serving.

Chef's tips

• 'Julienned' means to cut carrots (or other vegetables) into thin strips, about 2–3 mm thick and 3–5 cm long. To save time, buy precut carrot sticks.

Pasta Salad
WITH SMOKED CHICKEN AND PESTO

 PREP TIME **10** MINUTES

 COOKING TIME **15** MINUTES

 SERVES **4**

2 cups uncooked pasta
1 cup cherry tomatoes, halved
2 smoked chicken breasts, cubed
1 cup black olives, pitted and sliced

BASIL & CASHEW PESTO

1 cup plain cashews
4 garlic cloves
2 Tbsp lemon juice
2 cups (± 80 g) basil leaves
½ cup (125 ml) olive oil
½ cup finely grated Parmesan-
   style cheese

1 Cook the pasta according to the packet instructions.
   Drain and set aside to cool.
2 Place the cooled pasta in a serving bowl with the cherry
   tomatoes, cubed chicken and olives.
3 Add the Basil and Cashew Pesto and stir through.
   Chill in the fridge before serving.

FOR THE PESTO

1 Place the cashews, garlic and lemon juice in a food
   processor and pulse until the cashews are finely chopped.
2 Add the basil and blitz until combined. With the motor
   running, slowly drizzle in the olive oil until you achieve
   a thick pouring consistency.
3 Add the grated Parmesan and process briefly, until just
   combined.

Chef's tips

• You can use any pasta shapes for the salad. For added colour, try
  tricolour fusilli (screws).

Potato Salad
WITH BACON

PREP TIME

5 MINUTES

COOKING TIME

15–20 MINUTES

SERVES

4

5 medium potatoes, peeled
   and cubed
1 litre water
8–10 bacon rashers

POTATO SALAD DRESSING
2 cups mayonnaise
2 Tbsp lemon juice
2 tsp Dijon mustard
½ cup chopped coriander
3 Tbsp grated Parmesan-
   style cheese

1 Place the potatoes and water in a pot and boil for
10–15 minutes, until tender when pierced. (Take care
that they don't break up, they should be just soft.)
Drain and set aside to cool.

2 Fry the bacon in a pan until crisp. Drain on paper towel,
then cut into bite-sized pieces.

3 Combine all the dressing ingredients in a serving bowl
and stir to mix.

4 Add the cooled potatoes and bacon and stir gently to coat.

Summer *Pasta Salad*
WITH OX TONGUE

PREP TIME

10–15 MINUTES
+ time to cook the pasta

SERVES

4–6

3 cups macaroni or pasta shapes

1 kg cooked ox tongue, sliced or cut into bite-sized pieces

1 cup cherry tomatoes, halved

1 cup black olives, halved and pips removed; brine reserved

1 cup cubed mozzarella cheese

Salt and ground black pepper to taste

Fresh coriander, roughly chopped

CORIANDER DRESSING

1–2 cups chopped fresh coriander

1 cup (250 ml) olive oil

¾ cup reserved olive brine

4 Tbsp red wine vinegar

2 Tbsp honey

Juice and grated zest of 1 lemon

2 garlic cloves, crushed or finely chopped

1 tsp Italian seasoning

1. Cook the pasta according to the package instructions. Drain and set aside to cool.

2. Place the cooled pasta in a serving bowl or platter. Add the ox tongue, tomatoes, olives and mozzarella. Season to taste with salt and pepper and toss lightly. Before serving, pour over the dressing and toss to combine. Garnish with chopped coriander.

TO MAKE THE DRESSING

1. Combine all the ingredients in a jug. Using a hand blender, pulse until emulsified. Set aside.

Roasted Butternut *and* Halloumi Salad

PREP TIME 10 MINUTES

COOKING TIME 40 MINUTES

SERVES 4

1 medium butternut, peeled
  and cubed (± 2 cups)
2 Tbsp butter
1–2 Tbsp brown sugar
150 g halloumi cheese, cubed
5 cups (± 80 g) rocket leaves
1 cup pickled red peppers,
  thinly sliced
½ cup pumpkin seeds
½ cup coconut flakes

OLIVE OIL & BALSAMIC DRESSING
½ cup (125 ml) olive oil
½ cup (125 ml) balsamic vinegar
1 tsp black pepper

1 Spread the butternut on a baking sheet. Dot with butter and sprinkle with brown sugar. Toss to coat, then roast in a preheated oven at 180°C for 30–35 minutes, until tender and starting to caramelize. Set aside to cool.

2 Pan-fry the halloumi in a nonstick pan until golden. Drain on paper towel. (*See page 133.*)

3 Place the rocket on a serving platter and top with the roasted butternut, fried halloumi and red peppers. Scatter over the pumpkin seeds and coconut flakes. Pour over the dressing just before serving.

TO MAKE THE DRESSING
1 Whisk the ingredients together in a jug or small bowl.

DRINKS

Umqombothi

You need plenty of time and a few large containers to make umqombothi,
or traditional African beer. It's a process that can't be hurried,
but the results will be worth the wait.

PREP TIME

60 MINUTES

MAKES

8-10 LITRES

+ 3 days
fermenting time

5 litres boiling water

2 kg maize meal

2 kg sorghum

2 litres cold water

1 kg extra sorghum

1   Bring 5 litres of water to the boil. Place the maize meal
and 2 kg sorghum into a large plastic bucket with a lid.
Add the water and mix well until you have a thick porridge.
To prevent any dust getting into the drink, rest the lid on top
of the bucket, but don't close it. Leave in a warm place for
2 days, to ferment.

2   After 2 days, pour the mixture into a large pot over low
heat. Stir in 1 litre of cold tap water and let it simmer for
1 hour, stirring often. Pour the cooked mixture into a clean
bucket or barrel and leave to cool. (Depending on the
weather, this could take a few hours.)

3   When completely cool, stir in 1 kg sorghum plus the
remaining cold tap water. Place a lid on the bucket and
leave it to ferment for one more day.

4   When bubbles form on the surface, the umqombothi is
ready. Strain the liquid through a large sieve into clean
bottles or jugs and leave to stand for a few hours to allow
any residual solid matter to settle. Store in the fridge for
up to 3 days.

Marula Beer

Called 'vukanyi' in isiSwati and 'emaganu' in Xitsonga, this recipe comes from the northeastern bushveld, where marula trees grow naturally. Everyone has heard stories about elephants getting giddy from eating fermenting marula fruits that have fallen to the ground. Because making beer is about controlling the process of fermentation (which determines the level of alcohol), how giddy you get is up to you!

PREP TIME

60 MINUTES

MAKES
4-5 LITRES

SERVES

UP TO **10**

+ 4 days
fermenting time

2 kg marula fruit
5 litres water
2 cups brown sugar

1   Wash the marula fruit well. Working over a bowl, cut the fruits in half and squeeze out the juice, pulp and pips. The skins can be discarded.

2   Add enough water to cover, then smash the peeled fruit thoroughly to separate the pulp from the stone (pip), which can be discarded. Using your hands, squeeze as much juice as possible from the pulp. You should be left with a thick liquid. If it is very sticky, add a little more water.

3   Add all the sugar and stir through. Cover the container with a lid or clean cloth, but don't seal it. Leave in a warm place for 4 days, to ferment.

4   Skim off any foam and pulp that has risen to the surface and discard. Strain or sieve the beer into clean containers. Serve immediately or store in the fridge for up to 3 days. (Don't keep it for longer, or it will start to go off.)

Chef's tip

• Marula fruits fall to the ground when they are ripe which is a good thing, as marula trees can grow to a height of over 15 metres in the wild! The season for fresh fruit runs from February to April.

Amahewu

This fermented maize-based drink is often made in summer,
as it is thirst-quenching. It tends to be low in alcohol,
and commercially produced versions are alcohol-free.

PREP TIME

60
MINUTES

MAKES

3½
LITRES

+ 2 days
fermenting time

4 cups super maize meal
500 ml cold water
3 litres hot water
1½ cups white sugar
3 Tbsp fine malt flour
   (sorghum malt)

1 In a large pot on low heat, combine the maize meal with
  500 ml cold tap water, stirring until you have a smooth,
  thick paste.
2 Increase the heat to high. Add 3 litres hot water, one cup
  at a time, stirring constantly to prevent any lumps. When it
  comes to the boil and thickens, reduce the heat to medium
  and simmer for 20–40 minutes, stirring constantly.
3 Remove from the heat and leave to cool completely. Once
  completely cool, add the sugar and malt flour and stir until
  the sugar is dissolved.
4 Transfer to a container, cover with a clean cloth, and leave
  in a warm place for 2 days to ferment. You need to stir the
  mixture periodically during this time.
5 Decant into bottles or jugs for serving (there's no need
  to strain it) and place in the fridge until cool. Serve chilled.

Ginger Beer

Homemade ginger beer is so different from commercial versions that you just have to try it. Unlike other home brews, it only needs to ferment for 24 hours, making it the perfect choice for those crazy weekends when the whole family decides to visit!

PREP TIME

45 MINUTES

MAKES

5 LITRES

+ 1 day
fermenting time

5 litres water

250 g fresh ginger, peeled
  and chopped

4 lemons or limes, peeled and
  juiced (retain the peel and pips)

2 cinnamon sticks

3 whole cloves

5 slices fresh pineapple

300 g sugar

1 sachet (10 g) instant dry yeast

1   In a large pot, combine the water with the fresh ginger, lemon or lime, peel and pips, cinnamon sticks, cloves and pineapple. Bring to a boil then lower the heat and simmer for 30 minutes.

2   Set aside until cool, then add the sugar and instant yeast. Stir well and cover loosely with a lid or clean cloth. Set aside in a warm place for 1 day to ferment.

3   Strain and decant into clean containers. Check for sweetness; if necessary, add small quantities of sugar syrup (*see* below) and stir in well. Place in the fridge to chill before serving.

Chef's tip

- To make a simple sugar syrup, dissolve 1 cup white sugar in 1 cup (250 ml) warm water over a low heat, stirring all the time. Allow to cool, then add to the ginger beer in small quantities, tasting as you go.

HOT GINGER, HONEY AND LEMON DRINK

PREP TIME

20 MINUTES

MAKES

2 LARGE MUGS

500 ml homemade
  ginger beer

2 Tbsp honey

1 Tbsp finely chopped
  fresh ginger

1½ tsp ground tumeric

1 slice of lemon

1   Place all the ingredients in a pot over medium heat and simmer for 15–20 minutes. Strain into a mug and drink hot. (You can reheat it in the microwave if necessary.)

RECIPE INDEX